THE CHILDREN'S
BIBLE

People were bringing little children
to Jesus to have him touch them, but the
disciples rebuked them. When Jesus saw this,
he was indignant. He said to them,

*"Let the little children come to me,
and do not hinder them, for the kingdom
of God belongs to such as these. I tell you the truth,
anyone who will not receive the kingdom of God
like a little child will never enter it."*

And he took the children in his arms,
put his hands on them and blessed them.

Mark 10:13-16 (NIV)

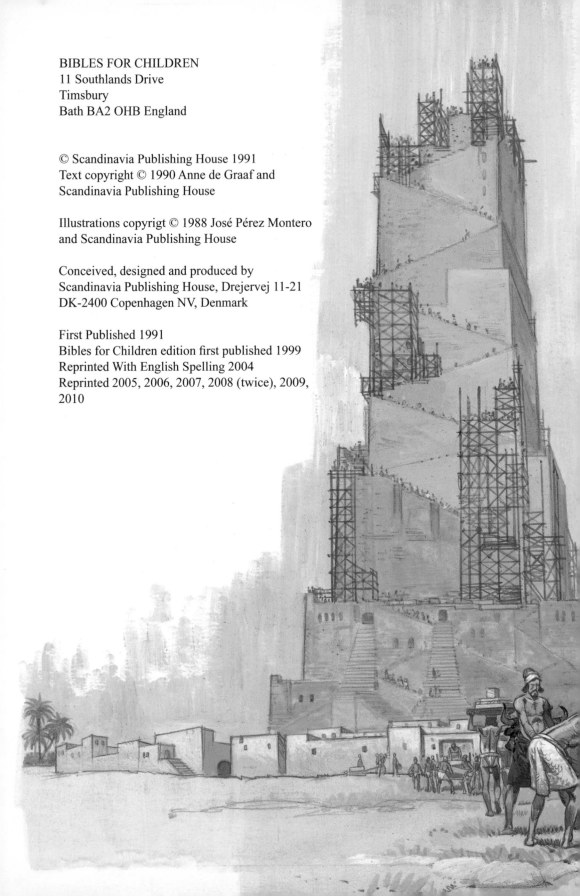

BIBLES FOR CHILDREN
11 Southlands Drive
Timsbury
Bath BA2 OHB England

© Scandinavia Publishing House 1991
Text copyright © 1990 Anne de Graaf and
Scandinavia Publishing House

Illustrations copyrigt © 1988 José Pérez Montero
and Scandinavia Publishing House

Conceived, designed and produced by
Scandinavia Publishing House, Drejervej 11-21
DK-2400 Copenhagen NV, Denmark

First Published 1991
Bibles for Children edition first published 1999
Reprinted With English Spelling 2004
Reprinted 2005, 2006, 2007, 2008 (twice), 2009,
2010

Bibles for Children is a National Charity registered with the Charity Commissioners of England and Wales (No. 1063200) and the Office of the Scottish Charity Regulator (No. SCO37757). It was etsablished in 1997 with the aim of advancing the understanding of the Christian religion through the provision of a Children's Bible to boys and girls in the Primary Schools of the United Kingdom.

Bibles for Children works closely with the Headteachers of Primary Schools and endeavavours to respond positively to requests for a Bible presentation. The number of Schools helped is only limited by the funds available. You are invited to share in the work by your prayers and gifts. The charity will be happy to provide fuller details of its activities on request, by writing to the charity's address at 11 Southlands Drive, Timsbury, Bath BA2 0HB or via the charity's website – www.biblesforchildren.org.uk.

Inquiries should be sent to:
Scandinavia Publishing House
Drejervej 15, 3. floor
DK-2400 Copenhagen NV
Denmark

My Family

Name
_____

Father
_____

Father's Parents
_____

Mother
_____

Mother's Parents
_____

Brothers & Sisters
_____

Brothers & Sisters
_____

Brothers & Sisters

THE CHILDREN'S
BIBLE

Retold by
Anne de Graaf

Illustrated by
José Pérez Montero

BIBLES FOR CHILDREN

CONTENTS

The New Testament

1

The Old Testament

God Makes Everything

Genesis 1:1-19

A long time ago there was nothing but darkness. It is hard to picture just nothing, but that is all there was . . . except for God.

So God made light. That way there could be day and night, instead of only darkness.

Then God made the earth and divided parts of it into oceans and seas and other parts into big pieces of land. God made all the plants and trees and made them grow on the land.

In the sky God made the stars and planets. He made the sun and moon so there would always be a day after every night.

It Looks Good

Genesis 1:20-25; 2:3-6

When God looked at all the water covering the world He made big fish and little fish. Some were too small to see.

For the sky He made large birds and small, in many colours. They were bright blue, dark green, brown, purple, red, black and white.

When He looked toward the land God saw grass blowing in the breezes and ripe fruit hanging from the trees. He knew it was a good place for animals. He made tiny bees and giant elephants, crocodiles, sheep and lions, all different sorts of animals. But they did not have names yet. There were just the right animals living in just the right places and not too many. And there was plenty of food and water for them all.

5

The First Man and Woman

Genesis 1:26-31; 2:1-7, 18-23

At that time there were no people on the earth. God wanted to make someone who was like Him. God put His hand in the dirt. He picked up a handful of dust, blew on it, then created a life that was the first man.

God brought all the different kinds of animals to Adam. "Call them whatever you want," God said. So Adam called one a hippopotamus, and another a butterfly. Once Adam had finished, God saw that not one of the animals was right for being Adam's special helper.

So while Adam slept, God took a part of Adam and around that part He made someone who was like Adam, but different. She was the first woman. When Adam woke up he was very happy. "Here is someone who can be my friend," he said. But she had no name.

When God finished making Adam and the woman, He was pleased. He decided He would rest for one day. He blessed all that He had made.

The Garden of Eden

Genesis 2:8-17, 24-25

God chose the prettiest part of the earth and gave it to Adam and the woman. It was a garden called Eden. In Eden all the animals lived peacefully with each other. No one was afraid.

Adam and the woman loved God very much. They walked around their garden with no clothes on because they had no reason to feel ashamed. For them there was one thing even better than all the dazzling flowers, tall trees and lovely smells in Eden. It was that they knew God loved them very much.

God told Adam and the woman they could do whatever they wanted. There was just one rule they must follow. God said, "You may eat fruit from any of the trees here except one. And that is the tree of knowledge of good and evil." The two people understood.

6

All for a Piece of Fruit

Genesis 3:1-19

Of all the animals in Eden the serpent was smarter and craftier than the rest. One day the serpent crept toward the woman. He teased her, "You don't have to listen to God. You can eat from that tree in the middle of the garden. You won't die!"

After this, the woman walked over to the tree. She did not know what she should do. Then she made a choice.

She picked a piece of fruit and took a bite. She brought the fruit to Adam and asked him to eat. Once they had both taken a bite they suddenly felt as if a cloud were hanging over them. The sunshine felt cold. For the first time ever, they were afraid.

They had done the wrong thing. The Lord was very sad because He must discipline His children. God did this because He cared. He wanted Adam and the woman to know that every choice was their own. Some choices lead to good things while other choices can be painful.

Out of Eden

Genesis 3:20-24

God told Adam and the woman that they must leave the garden of Eden. Otherwise, He said, they might disobey again and eat from another forbidden tree, the tree of life.

Adam and the woman looked at each other. They were together, but they still felt frightened of all that lay ahead. When they left Eden they would have to work hard to find enough to eat.

Adam gave the woman a name then. He called her Eve, which meant "Living."

Adam and Eve bowed their heads. They felt very sad. They knew God would continue to show His love for them. But the worst part of their punishment was that they would never be as close to God as they had been before they chose to disobey Him.

Two Brothers

Genesis 4:1-2

After Adam and Eve left Eden, they took care of each other. Soon their first child was born. They named him Cain. Later they had a second little boy. They named him Abel.

Cain and Abel helped their parents live in the world outside Eden. There they had to work hard to make sure they had enough to eat.

Cain's way of helping the family was to grow crops. He looked forward to the rain which watered the seeds he had planted. The grain he grew could be ground into flour for making bread.

He also gathered vegetables and fruit.

Abel's way of helping was to raise sheep and goats. He would milk the goats or sometimes kill them for the meat.

The First Murder

Genesis 4:3-16

One day Cain put together some of the crops he had grown and offered them to say thank you to God. Abel did the same, but he chose the best of the fattest of the lambs to give back to God.

God looked at the gifts both boys were offering Him. He liked Abel's gift better than Cain's.

This made Cain angry. He did not think God was being fair. God told Cain he could choose to do right or wrong. Cain chose to be angry.

He came up with a plan. He called Abel out to the fields. There, Cain did something very bad. He killed Abel.

God called him, "Cain, where is your brother Abel?" Cain shook his head.

God said, "You have done wrong. As your punishment, you will no longer be able to grow your crops. I am sending you far away from here." So Cain had to live in the land of Nod, which meant "Wandering."

Noah Builds a Boat

Genesis 6:5-22

Many, many years passed. After so much time, most of the people living on the earth chose not to care about God any more. They no longer taught their children to thank God. Over and over again they chose to hurt and lie and do wrong.

God looked at the people and grew very sad. He saw all the pain they caused each other. He wished He had never created people with the rest of the animals on earth. God decided He would take away the lives on earth which He had made.

At this time, when so many were bad, one man was different. His name was Noah. Noah often asked God's help. Noah listened for God's answers and then obeyed Him. This pleased God.

God told Noah, "I am going to put an end to all people. I will cause a huge flood to cover the land and everyone will drown. But I will spare you and those you love. Build a big boat, and build it the way I say. Then fill it with two of every type of animal. Fill it with food. Then you will be safe."

Noah trusted God. God gave Noah the plans for making the boat which was called an ark.

The Voyage of the Ark

Genesis 7:1-16

When the ark was finished Noah's family climbed in and left the door open. Soon animals and birds and all creeping creatures came crawling their way to Noah's ark. What a sight it was! And the noise was enough to bring Noah's neighbours out to watch and shake their heads all over again.

There were lions roaring, donkeys braying, dogs barking, birds singing and sheep bleating. Two by two, the animals entered the ark, all different types and shapes and sizes. Tiny worms wiggled, horses pranced and rabbits hopped.

After all the animals were inside, God closed the door to the boat, and quickly locked it so no one would fall out. And then it began to rain. It rained and rained and rained.

13

The Rescue

Genesis 7:17-8:1

It rained and rained and rained and rained. The water poured out of the skies. For forty days and forty nights the rains fell. Noah's ark rose higher and higher. The water lifted it right up over the mountains.

As the land flooded, all the living things on earth drowned. All the people and animals and birds died. There were no dry places on which to live. The water was everywhere.

The days dragged into weeks. Noah and his family stayed inside and the sun could not shine since dark rain clouds blocked its light.

God did not forget His promise to Noah. When the forty days were over, God sent a wind over the earth.

The End of the Storm

Genesis 8:2-9:17

Noah woke up to darkness. What was different? Then he knew. Noah could hear the waves slapping the sides of

the great boat. Always before the sounds of rain had kept him from hearing the waves. The rains had finally stopped!

Noah ran through the boat, waking everyone up. "It's over! The flood is over! Oh, let's thank God for ending the storm!"

But it took several more months before the land was dry enough to let the animals out. They tossed their heads and made even more noise leaving than they had when they got on. Shrieking and snorting, mooing and mewing, two by two they charged down the gangplank and made their way across the land.

Noah and his family thanked God for taking care of them.

When God heard their thanks, He promised never to destroy all living creatures again. Then God looked for every colour He could find and built the first rainbow. "As a sign of My promise never to flood the whole earth again, I have set My rainbow in the clouds."

15

The City Builders

Genesis 10:1-11:4

Noah's sons had many children who had many children who had many more children. The families spread out across the land. They learned how to farm, raise animals and build great cities.

Because they all came from the same family, all the people spoke the same language. When a stranger came from far away, everyone could know what he said.

Some of the people plotted together, "Let's build the biggest and best city ever built so we can be famous. Then we won't have to wander anymore. We will finally have a home."

The people were clever. Instead of using stones, they made bricks. They stuck the bricks together with tar, instead of mortar. Their walls were the strongest and highest ever. And they were very proud of themselves. They chose not to thank God for the things they used for building.

"We are so smart," they said.

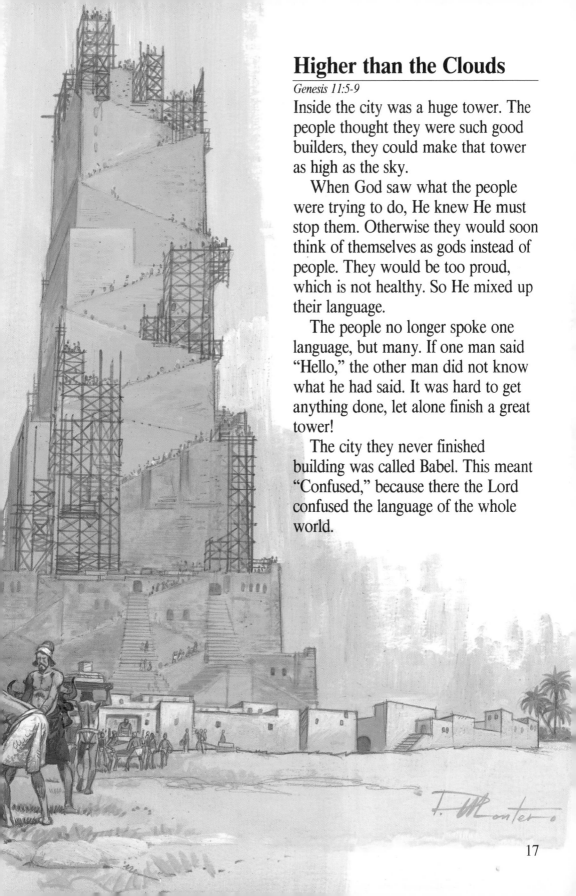

Higher than the Clouds

Genesis 11:5-9

Inside the city was a huge tower. The people thought they were such good builders, they could make that tower as high as the sky.

When God saw what the people were trying to do, He knew He must stop them. Otherwise they would soon think of themselves as gods instead of people. They would be too proud, which is not healthy. So He mixed up their language.

The people no longer spoke one language, but many. If one man said "Hello," the other man did not know what he had said. It was hard to get anything done, let alone finish a great tower!

The city they never finished building was called Babel. This meant "Confused," because there the Lord confused the language of the whole world.

17

God Chooses Abram

Genesis 12:1-9

Many, many years later there lived a man and his wife named Abram and Sarai. They were happy, except for one thing. They wanted very, very much to have a baby. But the years went by and none came.

One night, Abram heard God speaking to him. "Abram, I will make your family very great. All people everywhere will be blessed because of you."

The Lord told Abram to leave his home. Abram did not know where the Lord would lead him, but he did what God said.

He told Sarai what had happened and she trusted, too. She ordered the servants to pack the tents onto the camels.

"But where are we going?" they asked.

"I don't know," she said, then smiled. If Abram could wait for God to tell them where they were going, so would she.

The Promise of God

Genesis 13:14-18; 15:1-21; 17:1-27

God led Abram and Sarai, all their camels, sheep, goats and servants to the land of Canaan. He told them "This is the land I will give to your children." But God did not want Abram to stop in Canaan. Not yet.

Abram and Sarai moved their tents to Mamre at Hebron. Year after year they wished for a child. Finally Sarai grew too old to have babies.

Then one night, Abram heard God say, "Look up and count the stars."

Abram saw stars blinking everywhere. "Someday there will be as many in your family as there are stars in the sky," God said.

Then God gave Abram and Sarai new names. Abram became Abraham, which meant "Father of Many." And Sarai became Sarah, which meant "Princess."

19

On the Way to Sodom

Genesis 18:1-33

A short time later, Abraham had three
visitors. Abraham knew that one of
the men was really the Lord. He
walked with the three to a hill. From
there they could look down at the city
of Sodom.

The Lord said, "I have heard how
terribly evil the people are who live in
Sodom. If it is true, then I will destroy
that place."

The two men who had travelled
with the Lord were really angels in
disguise. They set off for Sodom.

Abraham wanted very much to ask
the Lord a question, but did he dare?
He knew, though, that the Lord was
his Friend, as well as
his God. So he

swallowed hard. "Lord, what if there are fifty good people in Sodom? What will happen to them?"

"I will not harm the city if there are still fifty good people."

Then Abraham asked again and again, each time using smaller numbers, would God spare the city for forty-five good people, for forty, thirty, twenty, or for ten? Each time the Lord said yes.

Lot Is Rescued

Genesis 19:1-29

There were not ten good people in Sodom, but four. The only bright spot in the evil city of Sodom was a man named Lot. Lot was Abraham's nephew. He lived in Sodom with his wife and two daughters.

Lot met the angels, who were disguised as men. "Come to my house. There you will be safe from the mean people here."

The people of Sodom tried to hurt the angels, though. The angels told Lot, "You must come with us. The Lord cannot stand this bad place. He's going to destroy it! We will help you run away, but you must not look back!"

Just a few hours later, the Lord rained fire onto Sodom. Lot and his family were safe, but Lot's wife looked back to watch. Instantly she became a tall stone!

God had kept His promise to Abraham. He took care of the good people in Sodom.

Isaac Is Born

Genesis 21:1-6

God had promised Sarah and Abraham a child and Sarah should not have worried. When the three strangers visited Sarah and Abraham, the Lord promised they would have a baby within a year.

Sure enough, in less than a year the impossible happened. Old Sarah, far too old to have children, gave birth to a son. Abraham was a hundred years old when Sarah's baby was born. He and Sarah were so happy, so thankful to God for finally answering their prayers, they cried for joy.

Every time Abraham saw the boy, he smiled. And Sarah smiled all the time. The child made them so happy, they would often laugh together. So they called the baby Isaac, which meant "He Laughs." The boy was a good reason to laugh and be happy.

Abraham and Isaac

Genesis 22:1-2

"Abraham!" The Voice of God called. "Take your son, your only son Isaac. I know how much you love him, and this is why I ask you to do this difficult thing. I want you to give Isaac back to Me."

Abraham said nothing. The God he knew would never want him to kill his own son. Abraham knew that. God had promised that Isaac would have many children. How could that happen if Isaac were dead?

It was like holding a friend's hand when you cannot see where you are going. The friend has said you are heading for a deep hole and you may fall into it. You hold on to the friend's hand anyway because it is the only guidance you can trust. Your friend will not let you down. Step by step, you follow him.

Abraham knew he could choose not to trust God. He could say no, run in fear and try and hide. But who can hide from God? Or he could choose to trust. Perhaps there was more to God's plan than what first seemed to be there.

True Trust

Genesis 22:3-8

Early the next morning Abraham woke his son up. "Come, Isaac, we are going on a trip."

Since Isaac was almost a young man by then, Abraham had Isaac carry the wood. He told his son they were going to make a sacrifice to God. Abraham carried the knife.

Isaac had often made burnt offerings with his father to give thanks to God. But this time was different. Something was missing.

"Father?" Isaac asked.

"Yes, my son?"

"I have the wood," Isaac said, "but where is the lamb which we usually offer?"

Abraham answered, "God will provide."

Saved in Time

Genesis 22:9-18

After three days of travel, Abraham said they had come far enough. Then

he told Isaac to climb onto the altar.

Isaac looked at his father. He saw in Abraham's eyes the love his father felt for him. Isaac chose to trust Abraham. As he lay himself down, Isaac asked God to keep him safe.

Abraham stood over Isaac, holding the knife up high. He was just about ready to kill his son when an angel said, "Abraham, Abraham!" Abraham stopped, his hand in mid-air. "Don't hurt the boy. You have shown how much you trust God with everything, even the life of your special Isaac."

Abraham looked and saw a ram whose horns were caught in a nearby bush. That was the offering God had provided.

The angel called down from the sky again. "Abraham, God says because you trusted Him so much, He will

make your family as many as the stars in the sky. All the other nations in the world will be blessed through you."

Isaac and his father hugged each other. Both father and son were happy just to be together.

Mission Impossible

Genesis 24:1-61

Many years later Abraham told his servant, "Go back to my homeland and find a wife for Isaac."

This was a nearly impossible mission. There were so many women. The servant prayed to Abraham's God all during the journey. Finally he arrived by a well in the land where Abraham once had lived.

He prayed, "Lord of my master Abraham, You choose the woman You know is right for Isaac. Show me clearly who she is. If I ask her for some water and she says, 'Drink, and I'll water your camels, too,' then I'll know she is the one."

Soon the servant saw a group of young women coming toward him. He asked one of them, "Please give me a little water from your jar." This was the test. What would she answer?

She said, "Drink, and I'll water your camels, too." The servant was very excited. It did not take long for the servant to explain his mission to her. He found out her name was Rebekah. Soon she was on her way to becoming Isaac's wife.

Rebekah

Genesis 24:62-67

On the day when the servant and Rebekah arrived, Isaac was meditating in the fields. He looked up and saw camels coming toward him. "Who is that beautiful woman there?" he wondered.

At the same time Rebekah looked toward Isaac. "Who is that handsome man?" she asked Abraham's servant.

"That is Isaac." She quickly covered her face with her veil. But her eyes shone when Isaac stopped her camel. It was love at first sight.

God had known just the right person to care for Isaac and just the right person to care for Rebekah.

Twin Brothers

Genesis 25:22-26

Isaac and Rebekah were married and lived happily together. But as the years went by they still did not have a little boy or girl. Rebekah and Isaac waited and waited until finally, Isaac prayed to God, asking Him to make it possible for Rebekah to have a baby.

A short time later, God answered Isaac's prayer, but not in the way he expected. There was not one baby growing inside Rebekah, but two! Twins!

The babies got bigger and bigger. Rebekah could often feel their little feet pushing against her. One night, Rebekah woke up suddenly. The babies had been kicking and hitting each other so hard, she hurt inside. She prayed to God, "Lord, are my babies all right? If I hurt when they push and shove, they must hurt, too. Why is this happening?"

God answered her, "The two boys you carry will some day become fathers of whole nations. One people will become stronger than the other. And the elder son will do what the younger tells him."

The time finally came for Rebekah to have her babies. The eldest, the first one to come out, was red. All of his little body was covered with hair. He was named Esau, which meant "Hairy."

A few minutes later, his brother was born. His tiny hand was holding onto Esau's foot. So his parents named him Jacob, which meant "He Grabs the Heel."

An Expensive Meal

Genesis 25:27-34

Many years passed and the boys grew up. They were both good at doing different things. Jacob was quiet, often helping at home and talking to his parents. Esau could hunt and catch wild animals.

One day, when Jacob was cooking a stew, Esau came back from hunting. He was very hungry because he had not eaten anything all day.

"Quick, give me some of that stew!" he said to Jacob. He sat down on the other side of the fire from Jacob. He could hardly wait for Jacob to dish up the stew.

Jacob listened to his elder brother talk about how hungry he was, and he thought of a plan. Jacob knew there was one thing Esau had that Jacob wanted, and that was Esau's birthright.

Because Esau was the eldest, Esau had a right to receive all of his father's riches and animals and servants after Isaac died. This right was called Esau's birthright. Jacob wanted that. So Jacob made a deal with Esau. "If you're really so hungry," Jacob said, "if you're really, really hungry, then sell me your birthright and I'll give you some stew."

Esau hardly heard what his little brother was mumbling about. Esau was hungry, he thought his stomach had shrivelled up and died. He did not care what he had to do, he wanted food. "Yes, all right, whatever you say. Give me some stew now!"

"Swear to it first," Jacob said. So Esau swore an oath to him, selling his birthright to Jacob.

Rebekah Is Cunning

Genesis 27:1-40

As the two brothers grew older, Jacob became Rebekah's favourite son. She loved Esau too, but she wanted only the very best for Jacob.

When Isaac had grown very old, he could no longer see. One day, Isaac told Esau, "My son, because you are the eldest, I want to give you my blessing. First, though, go hunting and cook some tasty meat for me. Then I will give you your blessing."

Rebekah had overheard what Isaac said to Esau. After Esau left, she said to Jacob, "Your father is about to give Esau his blessing. I want that for you. Go and kill two of our best goats. I will fix them just the way Isaac likes his meat. Then you can bring it to him and you will get his blessing instead of your brother."

Jacob did as he was told. When the food was ready, Rebekah glued goat fur to Jacob's neck and arms and hands so his skin would feel like Esau's hairy skin. Jacob went into his father's room.

"How did you find the food so fast, my son?" Isaac asked.

"The Lord helped me."

"But you sound like Jacob. Come here," Isaac said. He ran his hands over Jacob and felt the hair of the goatskin. "You feel like Esau, though," he said.

Then Isaac tasted the food Jacob gave him. "Ah," he said. "Here is your blessing."

A blessing was a very special thing. Isaac knew God was listening. He asked Him to make his son rich and to have other people, including his brother, serve this son. He asked God

to bless all the people who were good to his son, and curse those who were mean. When Isaac finished praying, Jacob left the room.

No sooner was Jacob gone, though, when Esau came back from his hunting trip! He rushed into his father's room, but Isaac said, "Why have you come back a second time?"

"But this is my first time," Esau said.

Isaac sighed. "That must have been Jacob then. Esau, your brother has stolen your blessing."

Esau was furious.

A Family Is Divided

Genesis 27:41-46

Esau could not believe his little brother had tricked him a second time! First, Jacob had taken his birthright, all the riches Isaac would have left him. Then Jacob had stolen

his blessing, God's protection for the future. Esau was so angry, he decided to kill his brother.

Rebekah found out about Esau's plan and warned Jacob. "You will have to go far away. Go and stay with my family," she told him. Jacob packed his things, quickly said good-bye, then disappeared into the desert.

By the time Esau heard about it, Jacob was long gone. He knew it was useless to try and follow. So Esau stayed with his parents, taking care of them in their old age.

Esau may not have had his father's blessing, and he may have been foolish enough to trade his birthright for a bowl of stew, but Esau knew it was an honour to take care of his parents as they grew older. Esau would keep the family strong until Jacob returned.

The Wrestling Match and Jacob's New Name

Genesis 32:1-31

After twenty years in his mother's land, the day finally came when Jacob thought he should go home. He had two wives, several children and hundreds and hundreds of sheep and goats.

As Jacob came closer and closer to home, he felt more and more nervous about Esau. Would his brother still be angry?

On the night before Esau was to meet Jacob, he felt very small. It was to become a night full of surprises, though, a night Jacob would never forget.

As Jacob stood alone under the stars, worrying and praying, a man came from out of the desert. It was dark and Jacob could not see who the man was. It was not Esau. Whoever it was, the man was very strong and he wrestled with Jacob.

All night long the two grabbed and grappled, rolling in the sand, over and

over again, panting and heaving. But neither seemed to win. They were of equal strength. Then the stranger touched the bones in Jacob's hip, causing one bone to come loose. Jacob hurt from the loose bone.

The strange man said, "Let me go, it will soon be sunrise."

Then Jacob knew who he was.

"This is no man," Jacob thought. "It is either an angel or ... could it be? It is the Lord God Himself."

"What is your name?" the stranger asked.

"Jacob."

"No, you are no longer Jacob. Your new name is Israel, because you have struggled with God and with men, and you have won," the stranger said.

"And what is your name, please?" Jacob said.

The stranger did not answer. He blessed Jacob. Suddenly, the stranger was gone and Jacob knew he had seen God face to face. The sky shone pink and gold as Jacob limped back to camp.

Fighting in the Tent

Genesis 37:1-4

Jacob finally did make it home and Esau had forgiven him, after all. Jacob arrived just in time to see his father before he died. Then Esau left to make a life for himself.

During the long journey home, though, Jacob's favourite wife Rachel had died. She left behind two sons, Joseph and Benjamin. Jacob's other wives had ten sons.

Jacob stayed in his parents' home, where he raised his twelve sons. Joseph and Benjamin were Jacob's favourites because they were Rachel's children. This made his other sons jealous.

One day Jacob made Joseph a very lovely robe. He called his son into his tent. "Here, my good son, this is for you," Jacob said.

Joseph gasped. It was special to have a new robe, but to have one like this, why, he had never seen such a robe before! "I do not deserve something as lovely as this."

"Don't be silly, Joseph. It's a gift. I give it to you because I want to."

Joseph took the beautiful robe. But when his brothers saw his gift, they grew even more jealous than before. "Why don't we get gifts like that?" they grumbled.

Joseph's Dream

Genesis 37:5-11

One morning, Joseph woke up with a start. He had had a very strange dream. It was so real, he felt he just had to talk to someone about it.

Joseph went looking for his brothers. "You'll never guess what I dreamed last night," he said when he found them.

Even though his brothers were mean, Joseph was so excited by his dream, he hardly noticed. He said, "I had a strange dream. We were all out in the field, tying the grain into bundles. Suddenly, my bundle stood straight up, while all your bundles came and stood in a circle around mine and bowed down to it."

His brothers grew angry. "Who do you think you are? You're not a king! There is no way any of us would ever bow down to you!"

A few days later Joseph had another dream. Again he told it to his brothers. "Listen," he said. "I had another dream and this time the sun and moon and eleven stars were bowing down to me." But this only made his brothers even angrier.

When Joseph told his father about his dreams, Jacob was stern with him. "Don't be too proud of yourself, Joseph," Jacob said.

In the Well

Genesis 37:12-24

Joseph sat on the ground, playing ball with his brother Benjamin. When Jacob saw the boys he said, "Joseph, I want you to go to where your brothers have taken the sheep to pasture. See if all is well, then come back and tell me what you have learned."

Joseph jumped up and hugged his father good-bye. Then he set out. "It's a good day for an adventure," he thought. Joseph walked and walked

and walked. After some time, he saw his brothers' camp just ahead.

When they saw him, though, they groaned, "Oh no, here comes that silly dreamer, Joseph. We know a way to get rid of him once and for all. Let's throw him into one of the wells near here. Then we can say a wild animal killed him. Ha! His dreams won't come true if he's dead."

"No wait," the eldest brother said. His name was Reuben. "Throw him into the well, but don't kill him. Not yet anyway." Reuben said this because he knew if he were the one to get Joseph out of the well, his father would think he was a hero.

When Joseph arrived, he panted up the last hill and smiled. He had finally found his brothers. But when he saw the looks on their faces, he stopped smiling.

His brothers formed a circle around him. He turned one way, then the other, then the other, but he was trapped. Before Joseph knew what was happening, they jumped all over him. They tore off his beautiful robe and threw him into a dark, dry well.

Joseph cried out, but it did no good. "Thump!" He landed in the dust and looked up. All he saw were his brothers' faces laughing as they dropped sand on him. He covered his face with his hands and moved up against the wall. When his brothers finally left, Joseph cried. Very quietly, he sobbed, wishing he were back home with his father and brother, playing in the sunshine.

On the Way to Egypt

Genesis 37:25-35

Later that day, one of Joseph's brothers had a terrible idea. Judah pointed at a caravan. "Do you see those slave traders? Let's sell Joseph to them." Reuben was not there to save Joseph. He was out watching the sheep.

When the slave traders arrived, Joseph's brothers pulled him out of the well. The traders paid twenty pieces of silver for Joseph. They strapped him on to a donkey, then rode off across the desert.

When Reuben arrived back at camp, he bent over the well. "Joseph," he whispered, "it's all right. I'll get you out tomorrow." Reuben still planned on becoming a hero. But he heard no answer. "Joseph!" he called out. Silence.

"Why are you talking to an empty well?" Judah laughed at Reuben.

"But, but, where is Joseph?" Reuben asked. "What have you done to our brother?" He grabbed Judah and shook him.

"Calm down," Judah said. "Here's your share." He gave two of the silver coins to Reuben.

"You sold him as a slave?"

"Yes. And by now our spoiled brother is on his way to Egypt." Judah grinned.

But Reuben knew how much Joseph meant to their father, Jacob. This news would break his father's heart.

The next day the brothers killed a goat and dipped Joseph's robe into the blood. They went back home and showed the robe to Jacob.

Jacob cried out, "My son's robe! Some terrible animal has killed him. Joseph must surely be dead!"

Joseph Must Work Hard

Genesis 37:36; 39:1-6

Joseph travelled with the slave traders a long, long way. "Lord God," he whispered in the hot sun. "I don't know what it will be like in Egypt. I may have to carry stones so the Egyptians can build their pyramids. But Lord, I know wherever I am, You will be there. Please help me."

At night while he stared at the stars, Joseph prayed for his family. "I think I know why my brothers did what they did. I was acting too proud. I'm sorry, Lord. Please take special care of my brother Benjamin. And please keep father safe so that someday I might see him again."

After many days of travelling, the caravan arrived at a big city. They sold Joseph at the slave market. When Joseph saw his new master, he knew God was taking care of him.

The man who bought Joseph was called Potiphar. He was rich, but more important, he was kind. Joseph would not have to haul bricks for the pyramids. Instead, he could work in Potiphar's house.

Joseph worked hard for Potiphar. He tried to find things which needed to be done. Every time he did a job, Joseph wanted it done right, so God would be pleased.

At first Joseph kept the house clean. Then he watched over the work in the fields and made sure the meals were cooked right. Soon Potiphar put Joseph in charge of everything he owned. All Potiphar had to do was decide what he wanted for dinner every night!

In Prison

Genesis 39:7-20

Joseph grew from a boy into a man while working for Potiphar. Every job he did, he did well.

One day Potiphar's wife looked out of her window and thought, "Oh, that Joseph is so handsome. My husband is gone on a trip for a few days. Maybe I can get Joseph to go to bed with me." She told Joseph to come to her bedroom.

When Joseph arrived, Potiphar's wife said, "Come to bed with me,

asking. But Joseph did not love her. Potiphar had trusted Joseph with so much. God would not be pleased if Joseph betrayed that trust.

Joseph shook his head no. "You are very beautiful," he said, "but it would not be right."

Potiphar's wife felt hurt that a slave would say no to her. She tried to force him to kiss her. He pushed her off and ran away. She tore Joseph's cloak away from him.

When Potiphar came home, his wife showed him Joseph's cloak. Then she told a lie, "Joseph attacked me! And you thought you could trust him. Ha! What kind of horrible man did you bring into our home?"

Potiphar believed his wife. He called the guards. He told them to put Joseph into prison. "And throw away the key!" he yelled as they dragged Joseph away.

Joseph. You are so good-looking and strong. Come kiss me."

Joseph knew that many men would like to do what Potiphar's wife was

The Dreams of Two Men

Genesis 40:1-23

Joseph stayed in the prison cell for many days. Then one morning two prisoners came to Joseph. They had a problem. "We had terrible dreams last night. Can you tell us what they mean?"

Joseph said, "I can't help you, but my God can."

The first man had been Pharaoh's cup bearer. He said, "In my dream I saw a vine. On the vine were three branches. As soon as the branches had little flowers on them, the blossoms became grapes. Pharaoh's cup was in my hand. I took the grapes, squeezed them into Pharaoh's cup and gave it to him."

Joseph said a quiet prayer, asking God for help. Then he knew the answer. "This is what your dream means. The three branches are three days. In three days Pharaoh will say you are free. But, please," Joseph added, "could you mention me to Pharaoh and get me out of this prison?"

The second man had been Pharaoh's chief baker. He said, "In my dream there were three baskets of pastries on my head. In the top basket were pastries for Pharaoh. Then birds landed on me. They ate the pastries which were meant for Pharaoh."

Joseph took a deep breath. God had shown him what the dream meant. It was not nice. "The three baskets mean three days. In three days' time Pharaoh will cut off your head and the birds will eat your dead body."

Three days later, it happened exactly as Joseph had predicted.

The Pharaoh's Dream

Genesis 41:1-8

Two long years went by. All that time Joseph heard nothing from Pharaoh's cup bearer. He kept busy taking care of the other prisoners. He shared his food with them and scrubbed the cells. Day in and day out he saw the sunshine stream through the barred windows. He prayed God might help him become free someday.

One morning in the palace, Pharaoh woke up yelling, "I've had such a bad dream! But it was so real, I'm sure it means something very important." Pharaoh looked at his servants. "Don't just stand there, find someone who knows what dreams mean!" he roared at them. The servants hopped away in fright.

All the wizards, magicians and wise men came. They listened as Pharaoh told them about his dreams. They looked at charts, drew pictures on their scrolls, then shook their heads. No, they did not know what the dreams could mean.

Fat and Skinny Cows

Genesis 41:9-32

The royal cup bearer stood next to Pharaoh. He made sure Pharaoh's cup stayed full of wine. It was not an easy thing to do when Pharaoh was so angry.

Suddenly, the cup bearer remembered a promise he had made. He felt terrible that he had forgotten Joseph for so long.

"Pharaoh," the cup bearer said. "When I was in prison, I made a promise to a Hebrew slave. He told me what my dream meant. I was supposed to tell you about him. I know he could help you now."

Pharaoh nodded. "Bring this prisoner to me." Two guards ran to fetch Joseph.

Joseph shaved and put on fresh clothes and went to see Pharaoh. Pharaoh said, "I had a dream and no one can tell me what it means. Can you?"

"No, I can't. But God can," Joseph said.

Pharaoh said, "In my dream I was standing by the River Nile. Then seven fat cows came out of the river. After them came seven thin and ugly cows. The seven ugly cows ate up the

44

seven fat cows. But when they were finished eating, they still looked as thin as before.

"But there is more. I also dreamed about seven full heads of grain. They grew on a single stalk. After them seven other heads sprouted, but they were withered and burned by the wind. The thin grain swallowed up the seven pieces of good grain. I told all this to the wizards. No one could tell me what it meant." Pharaoh looked at Joseph.

Joseph stared at the ground. He prayed, "Please God, what does it all mean?" Then he knew. Just like that, God opened Joseph's mind. He knew what the dreams meant.

"Pharaoh, the two dreams mean the same thing. There will be seven years of plenty to eat and drink. All the poor will be fed. But after those seven years will come another seven. Then the crops will not grow. All the food will run out. Everyone will go hungry during those years."

Joseph told Pharaoh these things would happen very soon.

Joseph Helps Pharaoh

Genesis 41:33-42:3

Joseph stood before the pharaoh. He took a deep breath. "Pharaoh should put someone in charge of all the food in Egypt. Store the extra away. When the crops fail, the people can eat the food in the storehouses. Then they won't have to go hungry."

Pharaoh called his advisers. They mumbled and nodded their heads, then mumbled some more. They stood back as Pharaoh spoke, "Your God is with you in a very special way. He helps you to see where others are blind. I feel I can trust you. You will be the man for this job. You will rule my house, my people and all the food stores in the land. There will be no one greater than you in all of Egypt, except for myself."

Joseph staggered back a step. Just that morning he had been a prisoner. Now Pharaoh was giving him an Egyptian name. It meant "God Speaks; He Lives," because Pharaoh knew God had spoken through Joseph.

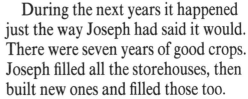

During the next years it happened just the way Joseph had said it would. There were seven years of good crops. Joseph filled all the storehouses, then built new ones and filled those too.

When the seven bad years came, Egypt was the only country with food. People from all over went there to find something to eat.

The famine, as the years without food were called, reached all the way into the land of Canaan. That was where Joseph's father and brothers still lived. They had grown rich during the seven good years. Once the seven bad years started, though, Jacob and his eleven sons ran out of food. Most of the sons were grown up and had families of their own to feed. Everyone was hungry.

The brothers grumbled, "What will we do now? Where will we find food?"

Jacob knew there was food in Egypt. He had heard that from some merchants travelling through the area. He told his sons, "If you don't want to starve to death, then go to Egypt. Take money with you and buy us some food."

The Brothers Learn Their Lesson

Genesis 42:4-38

The brothers loaded up their camels and donkeys. They rode off toward Egypt. Not all of Jacob's sons left, however. Benjamin stayed at home.

Benjamin was Jacob's favourite son. After losing Joseph, Jacob never let this last child of Rachel's out of his sight. Jacob still missed Joseph terribly. But Benjamin made his father laugh and smile. "No," Jacob thought, "Benjamin must stay here with me. What would I do if I lost Rachel's second child as well as her first?"

Together Benjamin and Jacob waved at the ten brothers. Soon all they could see was a cloud of dust. Jacob took Benjamin's hand. The father and son began to pray. They prayed for the ten brothers. They prayed they would be kept safe and would come home soon.

When the brothers arrived in Egypt they went straight to the man in charge of selling grain. That was Joseph. They did not see who he was. Joseph looked and acted too much like an Egyptian.

Joseph knew who they were, though. Yet he did not tell them. Instead he called them spies.

"We're not spies, we're brothers!" they told him. "There were twelve of us, but one is gone and the youngest is with our father."

"I don't believe you," Joseph said. "If you're not spies, then prove it by going home. Bring the youngest to me. In the meantime, I will keep one of you as prisoner." Joseph pointed at his brother Simeon.

The brothers stood with their mouths open. Then Joseph said, "But first you all must spend three days in prison."

When the three days were over, nine of the ten brothers rode home.

On the way they discovered that the money they had used to pay for the grain had been given back to them. "Oh no," they moaned. "The Egyptian will think we stole the grain."

When the brothers arrived home, they told Jacob what had happened. They asked if they could take Benjamin back to Egypt.

"Absolutely not! No one is taking my Benjamin from me. No. Benjamin stays here." Jacob would not even listen to the brothers. He thought, "It is bad enough that Joseph is dead. Now they have left Simeon behind. No, they will never take Benjamin away."

Benjamin May Go Along

Genesis 43:1-34

Slowly but surely, the grain from Egypt ran out. Soon there was hardly anything left. Jacob and his sons and their wives and children cut back from three meals a day to two. Soon they could only eat one meal a day.

Again and again the brothers had asked Jacob to let them go back to Egypt. After all, Simeon was still there. But Jacob always said no. He knew it would mean saying good-bye to Benjamin.

Finally he had no choice but to think of his large family. So he said yes. And Judah, the brother who had sold Joseph as a slave, said he would take special care of Benjamin. "Nothing will happen to him," he promised.

"Just to make sure," Jacob said, "bring twice as much money. That way you can pay the Egyptian back for the last load of grain. Take him gifts of honey, perfume, pistachio nuts and almonds."

As soon as the brothers arrived in Egypt, they went to Joseph. All he could do was stare at his brother Benjamin. He had grown into a handsome young man.

"Come, stay in my house and we will have a big meal together," Joseph said. Then he had Simeon brought out of prison. When the brothers arrived at the house, they told the steward about the money they had found on their trip home. He reassured them and they went inside.

"How is your father?" Joseph asked. He held his breath.

"He is alive and well," the brothers answered.

Joseph looked at Benjamin again. He reached out a hand and put it on his head. "May God be good to you, my son," he said. Suddenly he turned away. His brothers were bowing down to him, just like in his dream so long ago.

The memories were suddenly too much for Joseph. He ran from the

room. Once alone, he cried and cried. "Lord," he prayed, "You have brought us together again. I love them all so much."

Joseph wiped away his tears. He went back to the brothers. It was a grand party and lasted most of the night. But never once did Joseph tell the brothers who he really was.

51

The Stolen Cup

Genesis 44:1-34

The next morning the brothers rode off for home. They were happy. They had rescued Simeon, bought food for their families and eaten with an important man. Best of all, Benjamin was safe.

Little did they know that Joseph had a plan. He had ordered a servant to hide his silver cup in Benjamin's bag. The palace guards were chasing them because of it.

They galloped alongside the brothers. "Get off your camels and donkeys," the guards ordered them.

"What have we done wrong?" Reuben asked.

"One of you has stolen our master's silver cup!"

"But why would we steal?" the brothers cried.

The guards went from camel to camel, donkey to donkey. They ended up at Benjamin's donkey. When they reached into his sack, a shout went up. The guard raised the silver cup into the air.

The brothers groaned. "Oh, no! This is terrible. Benjamin what have you done?"

Benjamin was so shocked, he just shook his head. "But, I didn't take it!"

The guards ordered them back to Joseph's palace. The brothers begged Joseph, "We never meant to take your silver cup. Please forgive us."

"You may go," Joseph said. "Only the thief must stay behind."

Judah said, "But our father will die if we don't bring Benjamin back to him. He has already lost one son. He could not bear to lose this one, too.

"Please, I beg of you, let me stay here in his place. Please. If Benjamin stays here, none of us can face our father again." Judah fell to his knees.

The Truth Comes Out

Genesis 45:1-24

Joseph looked at Judah on his knees. He saw how scared Benjamin was. Then he told the servants, "Leave us. I want to be alone with these men!"

The servants left the room. Joseph said, "I am your brother Joseph." They did not believe him. They were so terrified, they could not look or listen. "Open your eyes," Joseph said. He came closer to them. "I am Joseph, the one you sold into Egypt!"

When Joseph said that, the brothers took a good look. Then they became even more afraid. If he really were Joseph, then he should kill them for what they had done to him.

"No, no, don't be afraid anymore, brothers. Don't be angry with yourselves. God sent me here to make sure there would be enough food for our family."

Joseph's brothers stared at him with big eyes.

"Don't you see?" he said. "You did not send me here, God did. God made me ruler of all Egypt, over everyone but Pharaoh. This was all part of God's plan for taking care of our family. Now hurry back to my father. Tell him to bring our whole family to Egypt and to hurry. I will make sure you have enough to eat."

Joseph threw his arms around Benjamin. He gave him a big bear hug and started crying. He was so happy to see him again.

When Pharaoh heard the news, he gave the brothers many carts so they could bring their wives and children and things back to Egypt. Pharaoh was happy for Joseph.

Before they left, Joseph gave the brothers many animals and other beautiful gifts. "Give them to my father," he said.

A Baby in a Boat

Exodus 1:1-2:4; 6:20

Joseph's family moved to Egypt. They lived there for hundreds of years. As they grew, Joseph's family became known as the Israelites, or Hebrews.

Four hundred years after Joseph brought his family to Egypt, a mean pharaoh ruled the land. He did not like the Israelites. Pharaoh made them all into slaves. Then he ordered that every Hebrew baby boy should be killed!

One mother of a little boy tried everything to keep her son alive. He was a beautiful baby with the wisest dark eyes. For three months she managed to keep the baby hidden. But she knew time was running out.

"There must be something we can do to save him," she cried to her husband. Night after night they prayed for an idea. Their children, Miriam and Aaron, prayed with them.

Then the family had an idea. The mother wove a basket together out of reeds. The basket became a little boat. Then they took the baby and wrapped him in soft blankets. They laid him into the basket.

Miriam and her mother brought the basket down to the river. They gently placed it in the water. "Watch him, Miriam," the mother said.

Saved by a Princess

Exodus 2:5-9

God had heard the prayers of the baby's family. He had very special plans for that boy. The basket floated down the river. Then one of the pharaoh's daughters, a princess, chose just that moment to go for a swim.

The princess stood in the water. She laughed with her servants. The sun shone and the birds seemed to laugh with her. The princess splashed one of her maids. Soon the girls were throwing water, giggling and chasing each other.

Suddenly, one of the servants saw the basket. "Princess, come look what the river has brought us," she called. She carried the basket up to the shore and laid it on the sand.

"Ahhhh," the girls sighed. There, inside the basket, was a beautiful baby. He had kicked off his blanket and was crying.

"He must be a Hebrew boy," the princess said.

She knew about her father's order to kill the Hebrew boys. That just made this baby all the more precious. "He's so hungry, isn't there anything we can give him?"

Miriam had been watching and praying. She wanted the princess to save her little brother. Now she ran up to the princess. "I know a Hebrew woman who could feed him. Do you want me to get her?"

"Yes, once he's old enough to eat on his own, you can bring him back to me."

So the baby went back to his family. There, his parents, brother and sister all loved and took care of him. They thanked God for answering their prayers.

Moses Strikes a Blow for Freedom

Exodus 2:10-14

When the baby was about three years old, his family brought him back to the princess. She smiled at him. "This boy will be my very own son."

As Moses grew older, he learned that he was Hebrew, not Egyptian. Whenever he saw how his people were treated like slaves, he felt angry. "It's not fair," he cried to the princess.

She said, "We can't question what Pharaoh does. He is king."

The years went by and Moses became a grown man. One day, he was walking in the streets when he saw an Egyptian beating a Hebrew slave.

"No!" he yelled. He hit him hard, pushing his head up against a wall. The Egyptian fell dead in the sand where Moses hid him.

The next day Moses saw two Hebrews fighting. "Don't," he said to one of them. "Why are you hitting him?"

The Hebrews looked at Moses' fine clothes. They laughed at him. "Who are you to tell us not to fight? Didn't you just kill an Egyptian yesterday?" They laughed. They knew as soon as Pharaoh heard what Moses had done, Moses would be killed.

Moses grew afraid. "If these two slaves know I killed that Egyptian, who else might know?" he wondered. "I must leave Egypt, and quickly!"

The Bush Which Caught Fire without a Match

Exodus 2:15-3:10

Pharaoh did find out about Moses' killing the Egyptian. His guards chased Moses into the desert, but did not find him. In the desert Moses met a wise man named Jethro. Moses married one of Jethro's daughters. During the next forty years he raised his family in the desert.

One day Moses was taking care of Jethro's sheep when he saw something very strange. At the foot of a mountain he saw a bush on fire. But the fire did not spread. The bush did not burn up.

Then Moses heard a Voice say, "Moses, Moses!"

"Here I am."

"Do not come any closer," the Voice said. "Take off your sandals. You are standing on holy ground. I am the God of your father, the God of Abraham, the God of Isaac and the God of Jacob."

When Moses heard this, he fell to the ground. He was afraid to look at God.

The Lord said, "I have seen how cruelly the Egyptians treat My people. The time has come for Me to rescue them. I will bring them back to the land I promised Abraham and Isaac so long ago. It is a lovely land, with plenty of water for crops.

"Go now, Moses. I am sending you to Pharaoh to lead My people, the Israelites, out of Egypt."

A Hundred and One Excuses

Exodus 3:11-4:9

Moses said, "Who am I? I'm not important enough to tell Pharaoh he should let our people out of Egypt."

God's answer to Moses was simple. "I will be with you."

Moses said, "But no one will believe I speak for You. How will I show the people who You are?"

God said to Moses, "I Am Who I Am. That is My name. Tell the people that. Tell them the God who chose them as a special people has sent you."

Moses was still not ready to do what God asked him. He made God angry by coming up with excuse after excuse. Moses said, "When I tell them who You are, they will not believe me."

"The older people, the leaders, will believe you," God said. "Just to prove that I am with you, ask Pharaoh if you may take the people on a three-day journey into the desert. Ask Pharaoh for just three days when the people can worship Me. When Pharaoh says no, then I can work miracles and strike down the Egyptians.

Moses said, "But what if they still do not listen to me?"

The Lord asked, "What is that in your hand?"

"My staff," Moses answered.

"Throw it on the ground," God said. When Moses did so, the staff became a snake and Moses ran from it. When God told him to pick it up again, Moses reached out and picked up the snake. Instantly, it became his staff again.

Pharaoh Says No

Exodus 4:10-5:2

Moses tried every excuse he could think of. When he told God he could not speak well, the Lord said his brother Aaron could speak for him. Finally Moses had run out of excuses. He bowed his head. Moses was God's chosen man.

After the bush stopped burning, Moses said good-bye to his family. He headed for Egypt. On the way, Moses met his elder brother Aaron.

When Moses and Aaron arrived in Egypt, they went to Pharaoh. They told him, "The Lord, the God of Israel says, 'Let My people go so they can worship Me for three days.'"

Pharaoh said, "No! Why should I obey this God? I will not let the people of Israel go!"

God Promises Action

Exodus 5:22-7:16

After Moses met with Pharaoh, he prayed to the Lord, "God I'm so confused. What should I do?"

God said, "Because Pharaoh will not let you go, I will do mighty works. They will know that I am God."

Pharaoh had said he did not know the Lord when Moses first went to him. Soon, though, he would know without a doubt who God was. It was all part of God's plan.

God told Moses, "Go back to Pharaoh and ask him again to let My people leave his country."

Moses argued with God. "Why should Pharaoh listen to me?"

God told him it was all right. He reminded Moses he would not have to do the actual talking. Aaron could speak for him. He warned Moses, though, that when Pharaoh did not listen, the Lord would act.

Moses and Aaron went back to Pharaoh. To prove they really spoke for God, they threw Moses' staff onto the ground. It turned into a snake. Pharaoh called his wizards. When they threw their staffs down they became snakes, too. Then Moses' snake ate theirs. Still, Pharaoh would not do as Moses asked. The Lord told Moses that because Pharaoh would not listen, the time had come for God to show Pharaoh His power.

Terrible Plagues

Exodus 7:17-10:29

When Pharaoh said no, God punished the Egyptians for not letting His people go.

God sent ten plagues to Egypt. Plagues are bad events in nature which happen to one area all at once. Pharaoh sent for his wizards and wise men to make the plagues go away. God only ended the plagues, though, whenever Moses prayed to Him.

During the first plague, water turned to blood. When Moses stretched his staff over the River Nile, it turned into a river of blood. All the streams and canals, ponds and puddles, filled with blood. The fish died and the river stank.

A week later God told Moses to ask Pharaoh again to let the Israelites go. He told Moses to warn Pharaoh if he did not obey, God would fill the Nile with frogs.

When Pharaoh said no, the frogs came by the thousands. They climbed out of the river and streams and canals and covered the land of Egypt. They even went into the houses. People woke up to the sounds of "rib-it, rib-it" right in their ears.

Pharaoh asked Moses to make the frogs go away. Moses prayed and the frogs all died. But Pharaoh still did not believe in God. He still would not let God's people go.

God sent gnats, tiny flies that bite. They were everywhere. The Egyptians had to cover their mouths whenever they talked. Otherwise the little flies got caught in their throats. Then God sent a plague of bigger flies.

God sent diseases which made the cattle sick. The skin on people and animals turn red and itched.

God sent hail and thunderstorms. The wind blew hard, and locust insects came in huge clouds. They ate every green leaf they found. Soon there was nothing left in Egypt except bare branches and twigs.

Lastly, God caused the light of the sun to go out for three days. Instead of night turning into day, it was night, night, night and more night.

God gave Pharaoh chance after chance. He would not change his mind. He still would not let the people of Israel go. After God made the sun go dark, Pharaoh was so angry he yelled at Moses, "Get out of my sight!"

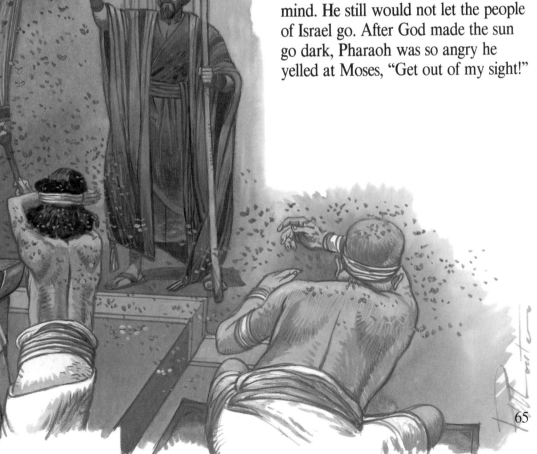

The Last Plague

Exodus 11:1-10

Pharaoh had not listened. God warned Pharaoh through Moses that He would send one last plague. After this tenth plague, Pharaoh would finally let the people of Israel leave Egypt.

Moses told Pharaoh, "The eldest son of all Egyptians, whether free or slave, will die. The firstborn of all your animals will die, as well. The children of the Hebrew families, though, will be safe. This is to show that God sees a difference between your people and His."

Pharaoh did not believe such a thing could happen. It would mean his own son would die. They would lose all the new calves and goats and sheep, too. Pharaoh trembled with rage. How dare this Hebrew threaten him that way?

Pharaoh decided not to believe in God's power. He closed his mind and told himself, "This could never happen."

"Out! Out of here!" he yelled at Moses. Moses left Pharaoh.

The Jewish Passover

Exodus 12:1-42

The people of Israel were scared. When they heard what God would do, they wondered, "How will we be safe?"

Moses told them God had given them special rules. On that night, whoever followed God's rules would be protected.

The night of the last plague was called "Passover" because that was when God "passed over" the people of Israel. He kept them safe. Moses told the people of Israel that they should always remember Passover night. They should tell the story of what happened to their children and their children's children, on down the years.

On the night of Passover, the people of Israel ate lamb and bread. Before the meal, they had painted the outside of their doors. They used the blood of the lamb they were to eat. That way, when the Lord passed through Egypt, He would know which homes to keep safe. He would know where the people of Israel lived.

One by one, as each Egyptian home discovered a dead child, a wail went up from all over Egypt. Every single Egyptian parent cried that night. And the people of Israel waited. They knew they were safe because they were God's chosen people.

When Pharaoh saw his eldest son dead in his bed, he knew he was to blame. None of this would have happened if only he had listened to Aaron and Moses.

Then Pharaoh ordered Moses and Aaron to come to him in the night and he told them, "Get out, you and the people and all your animals!"

The knock came on the Israelites' doors. "Now, it's time." They picked up their things and slung their babies onto their backs. They gathered their belongings, their cattle and sheep and left Egypt. They were on their way to God's promised land.

God Leads the Way

Exodus 13:17-14:13

All the people of Israel gathered in
one place. God showed the way in the
daytime by a pillar of cloud. They left
together and followed it. In the
night time it became a pillar of fire to
give them light. This way the people
always knew which way to go.

God led them along the desert road,
toward the Red Sea. The Israelites
were a great crowd of people. They
spread out on both sides of the road.
As they herded their many animals

before them, dust rose into a big cloud.

Back in Egypt, though, Pharaoh had changed his mind. "Who will do all the building and make all the bricks?" he asked himself.

Then Pharaoh took six hundred of his best chariots and the best men in his army. They charged after the people of Israel.

"Make camp on the shores of the Red Sea," God told Moses. "Pharaoh will think he has you trapped between the water and his army. But this will be another chance for Me to do a mighty work. The Egyptians will know that I am God."

The people of Israel set up camp where Moses told them. But something was wrong. Those on the outskirts of the camp could feel the ground shaking. They looked up and saw a cloud of dust coming closer. A cry went up, Pharaoh was hunting them down! There they were, with nowhere to go but into the water. "We're trapped!" they cried out.

They yelled at Moses, "What have you done to us? You brought us out of Egypt just so we could be killed in the desert? We would rather have stayed as slaves! At least then we would still be alive!"

Moses told them, "No, we're not trapped. God will fight for you. All you have to do is be still. Trust Him."

The people did not believe Moses. They panicked. They ran from one end of the camp to the other. They paced the shore like caged animals. Some of the men tried to come up with plans to get all the people across the water. The children started yelling and running around. The babies cried. The women watched the chariots coming closer and closer. In no time at all Pharaoh and his six hundred chariots would be right on top of them!

A Wall of Waves

Exodus 14:14-31

Moses tried to calm the people.
"Don't worry," he said. "Today you
will see God in action." The people
were too scared to listen.

God said, "Why do you cry out like
that? Moses, raise your staff and the
sea will split. There will be a wall of
waves on both sides. The water will
not touch you. Pass through the sea
with the people. I will protect you.
When the Egyptians try to follow, I
will make the water crash in on them

70

and they will die."

Moses raised his staff. A strong east wind blew the water so it stood straight up. A path formed in between the two walls of water! In the darkness, the people and all their sheep and cattle ran between the waves. They could hardly believe what was happening.

In the morning they were safe on the other side. When Pharaoh woke up, he shouted, "If they can cross dry land in the middle of the sea, so can I!"

Pharaoh and his troops plunged onto the path. They were halfway between shores when God told Moses to raise his staff again. Moses did, and with a mighty crash the water plunged back down!

Pharaoh, his six hundred officers, all the chariots, horses and other soldiers were swept away in the flood. At first the people of Israel heard their cries. Then all they saw were the dead bodies, washed onto the beach.

The people of Israel saw the great power of the Lord. They said, "Yes, God will be our Leader!" The long journey ahead of them no longer looked so terrible.

Nothing to Drink

Exodus 15:1-27

When Pharaoh and his men were drowned, the Israelites sang and danced. They were so happy to be safe. Miriam, Moses' sister, led the women in a dance. They went in and out, weaving their way between the campfires. She played the tambourine as all the women followed her.

Moses sang a song about God's mighty power and strength. Moses thanked God for saving His people and for bringing them out of Egypt.

Soon the day came for them to start travelling again. They followed God's pillar of cloud.

For three days they wandered through the desert. All that time they could find no water to drink. They stopped by a pool of sour water. If they drank that water, it would make them sick. To see the water and know they could not drink, just made the people all the thirstier.

Two million thirsty people began to grumble. They yelled at Moses, "What have you done to us? Here we are in the desert. We're dying of thirst. We could have been home, safe in Egypt. At least there we had water and fruit and fish. Here we have nothing!" Already the people had forgotten God's promise to care for them.

Moses called out to God. The Lord showed him a piece of wood. Moses threw the wood into the pool. The water became sweet and fresh. The people dashed into the pool, splashing and laughing. Now they could drink their fill.

Moses told the people, "Always remember, the Lord does take care of you." As if to prove this, God led the people to where water came out of the ground in twelve different places. There were palm trees to shade their tents. It was a perfect place to set up camp. The Lord had taken care of them again.

74

Nothing to Eat

Exodus 16:1-36

Soon it was time to break camp and travel on. Before long, the people were complaining again. They did not like the hot sun. They did not like the lack of water and food. The babies cried, the women moaned and the men grumbled.

When they had been out in the desert for about two months, the Israelites ran out of food. They yelled at Moses, "What have you done? There is nothing out here. Now we will all die. It's all your fault!"

Moses said, "God will take care of you. Trust Him!" They would not listen. They were stubborn and wanted to feel sorry for themselves.

Then the Lord spoke to Moses. "I will give the people bread in the mornings and meat in the evenings. They will rely on Me for what they need. They will learn to trust."

The next morning, the ground was wet with tiny drops of dew. When the sun dried the dew, the people saw small white flakes of bread resting on the ground.

In the evening a flock of quail birds landed around the camp. The people were able to catch as many as they needed. They roasted the birds and ate the meat. Thanks to God, for as long as they would travel through the desert, the people would always have enough to eat.

God on the Mountain

Exodus 19:1-25

The people of Israel travelled through the desert for three months. When they arrived at a mountain called Sinai, they set up camp. The women were glad to rest. They took care of the children. The men counted the animals, then set up the tents. Soon the smell of food filled the air.

In the evening Moses wandered among the families. The children ran up to him and he gave them all a pat on the head. After Moses greeted the people, he turned toward the mountain. Moses knew God wanted to meet him there. It was time.

As Moses climbed the cliffs, he heard God calling to him. "Moses, tell the people that if they obey Me, they will be My special people."

Moses climbed down the mountain. He called the leaders of the people together. He told them what God had said. There was a great crowd. The men all held torches as Moses spoke to them. "The Lord God has chosen you. Will you follow Him? Will you obey Him?"

A loud cheer rose from the crowd, "We will do whatever the Lord says!"

A few days later Moses and Aaron climbed the cliffs. The mountain was covered with smoke. There was a sound like a huge trumpet playing from the cloud. The people could hear the blast but could not see where it came from. They trembled in fright. This was a great moment for the people of Israel. God had come to meet them.

The First Ten Commandments

Exodus 20:1-21

Once Moses and Aaron were on the mountain, God came down to meet them. He came in a cloud of smoke and fire. God wanted to give the people a set of laws, or commandments. They could learn and shape their lives around these rules. Then they would know the difference between right and wrong.

God gave Moses the Ten Commandments. "Tell the people," God said, "I am the Lord your God. I brought you out of Egypt, where you were slaves. Worship no one but Me. I will be your only God. Do not make statues and worship them.

"Do not swear, do not say My name just to impress other people. Only use My name when you are praying.

"Keep the seventh day in the week for resting. Do not work on the Sabbath.

"Listen to what your father and mother say. Show them respect and honour. Never, ever make fun of them.

"Never kill another person. Never try to take a man or woman away from his wife or her husband.

"Do not take anything which is not yours. Do not lie or say false things about someone else or make things up. And do not spend all your time wishing for things you do not have."

As God finished speaking, a sound like great trumpets filled the air.

God Cares for His People

Exodus 20:22-31:18

Moses stood face to face with God. God and man were together. God loved Moses very much. He wanted His people to know how much He cared for them, too.

God said, "I will keep you healthy. You will have many children. That way you will be strong when I lead you to the promised land."

Moses had been deep inside the dark cloud, talking to God for a long time. A few times he went down to check on the people. When God said He wanted to give Moses the Ten Commandments written on stone, Moses stayed on the mountain.

Moses stayed with God for forty days and forty nights. All the people waited, and waited, and waited.

When God finished telling all these things to Moses, He gave him two flat pieces of stone. God had written the rules on these stones Himself.

The Golden Calf

Exodus 32:1-35

When Moses turned to leave, God spoke suddenly, "A terrible thing has happened! The people have forgotten their promises already. They are worshipping a golden calf."

The people had waited and waited for Moses to come down from the mountain. When Moses still did not show up, they decided he must be dead. Once again, they chose not to trust in God. They asked Moses' brother Aaron to make them another god. Aaron had taken their gold bracelets and rings. Using the melted gold he made them a golden calf.

God became very angry. He told Moses, "I will kill them all. I will start again in making a special people."

Moses begged God not to kill them. Then he started down the mountain. He carried the stone tablets God had given him. The closer Moses came to the camp, the more noise he heard.

Then he saw the golden calf, gleaming in the sunshine. "You are a terrible people!" he screamed at them.

The music stopped and the people stood still.

"How could you do this after all the Lord has done for you!" Moses yelled. In his rage, he flung down the stones with God's handwriting on them. He dashed them onto the ground with a mighty crash. They broke into a thousand tiny pieces.

Moses punished the people. Then he went back up the mountain. God told Moses that the people of Israel did not make Him smile like they used to. God was very, very disappointed.

The Second
Ten Commandments

Exodus 33:1-34:35

Moses pleaded with God to forgive the people of Israel. God said because Moses was the one asking, He would listen. Because God and Moses were friends, He would remember His promises to the people.

Moses was best friends with God. He asked God, "Show me Your ways." God told him that he would die if God let him see and learn everything there is to know about God. It would be too much.

God did say, however, that Moses could return to the top of Mount Sinai. There God would pass by so Moses could see more of God. This would be the closest anyone had ever come to God!

Moses climbed back up the mountain. The Lord came down from the cloud to be with Moses. Moses fell onto the ground. God's glory was too great. Moses kept his eyes shut tight and said over and over again how great God was. Again he begged God to forgive the people and still make them His chosen children.

God said He would. And then He made a great promise. For the second time, God told Moses all the laws for the people. He promised to bring the people of Israel to the land He had told Abraham would belong to his children.

God gave His rules and laws for the second time. Moses chiselled out the stone and God wrote down the Law again. Moses stayed up on the mountain forty days, just as He had the first time God gave him the Ten Commandments.

After the forty days were over, Moses climbed down the cliffs. He came back to the camp. This time the people had kept their promise. They had waited for him to return. They had been good.

83

Within Sight of the Promised Land

Numbers 13:1-30

The people travelled many months in the wilderness. One day God said to Moses, "Send spies into Canaan, the country I am giving you. Tell them to see what sort of land it is. Find out what the people are like who live there."

Moses did as God asked. He chose one man from each of the twelve tribes of Israel. Moses raised his hand and blessed the twelve men as they left camp.

After many, many days the men returned. One was Caleb and another was Joshua, the general. Caleb and Joshua told Moses, "Oh yes! You should see the land. It's so beautiful, with strong trees, and gentle hills. Flowers bloom everywhere and the crops are rich and plentiful. It really is as God promised, a land of milk and honey."

There was only one problem. The people who lived on the land were all very good fighters. Joshua and Caleb knew that with God's help, they could drive those people out of the land.

Not everybody agreed with Joshua and Caleb, though. Some of the other spies were troublemakers. In the end, they spoiled the trip for everyone that day.

We Are Not Strong Enough

Numbers 13:31-14:12; Deuteronomy 1:19-33

The other spies disagreed with Joshua and Caleb. They did not trust God to help them win their battles. They thought the tribes in Canaan were too dangerous to fight.

The Israelites believed these other men instead of believing God's promises. "Oh Moses!" they cried. "What have you done?"

Moses groaned. The people were complaining again! "Moses, we want to go back to Egypt!"

"Moses, it was your idea to leave Egypt in the first place. We should never have listened to you. Look, now we will die and for what?"

Moses and Aaron fell to their knees. They begged the people to trust God. Joshua and Caleb ripped their clothes. They swore God's promised land was a good place to live. But the people would not listen. They were very stubborn. They liked feeling sorry for themselves.

The Forty-year Punishment

Numbers 14:13-45; Deuteronomy 1:34-46

Once again God forgave the people. But they had to pay for being so stubborn. Too often they had not believed God or trusted Him. Because of this God said they would never reach the promised land.

"These people must wander in the wilderness," He said. "They will all spend the rest of their lives in the desert, all of them except Caleb and Joshua, who believed Me. I could have brought them to the promised land within a year. Instead, the people will wander in the desert for forty years. They will die in the desert. Their children will be the ones to finally settle in the land of milk and honey. This is their punishment."

When the people heard this, they cried out loud. It was too late, though. God had made up His mind.

Despite God's punishment, the people decided since the land was so close, they should go and fight the tribes anyway. They had forgotten that God had just said they would not be the ones to drive the tribes away. Their children would do that.

The people went off to battle, but they lost. Many men died in a battle which God had not helped them win.

For the next forty years the people of Israel would wander from place to place. The Lord did not stop leading them, but He did not lead them straight to the promised land. Their punishment was real. They had to spend the rest of their lives walking in circles, so close to Canaan, but never able to enter it.

The Choice of Life or Death

Deuteronomy 29:1-30:20; 31:2

Moses was over a hundred years old. He called all the people together one last time. He knew he would soon die. He called out in a mighty voice, "You have a choice! All of you who want to live, raise your hands!"

The crowd mumbled, "What does he mean?"

"Of course, we want to live!"

"Yes, yes!" they called. They all raised their hands.

"All those who want to die, raise your hands!" Moses called.

The crowd quickly lowered their hands. A silence fell over them. They waited. Somewhere in the crowd a baby cried.

"Today," Moses shouted, "you have said you choose life, not death. God wants to make a promise to you. He wants to give you food and water,

good land and large flocks. This is life. He wants to give you peace. He will give you all these things if you obey His laws.

"But if you do things on your own, if you grow proud, if you forget how God brought you out of Egypt, then you will be ruined! Do you believe me?" Moses paused.

"Yes, Moses, we will obey!" the people shouted back. Moses bowed his head and prayed it would be so. He loved the people very much, even if they had caused him so much trouble.

The Song and Last Days of Moses

Deuteronomy 31:1-34:7

Before Moses died, he wrote a

beautiful song for his people. He knew he was going to a different sort of promised land than Canaan. He was going to be with his best Friend, God.

Moses' song was all about the love of God. It told how faithful God had been through the years, of His power and might.

When Moses had finished singing, he felt very tired. Moses wanted so badly to see the promised land. He asked God if his time had come.

"Yes," the Lord said, "you can see the land now, but you will not cross into it. Go up Mount Nebo. From there you will see the land of Canaan." When Moses reached the top, he looked across the Jordan River. There was the promised land.

Moses stood on that hill for many hours. He stood and stared. His eyes drank in the sight of God's land. Wild flowers covered the hills. Tall trees swayed in the breeze.

Moses said, "Thank You, Lord." It was enough just to see the land.

While Moses gazed at the land which would soon belong to his people, he died. He died a strong man, still able to see and think clearly. God buried Moses in a valley near the mountain. Moses was the friend of God.

I Spy the Enemy

Joshua 2:1-3

When Moses died, Joshua became the leader of God's people. Once they were camped on the shores of the River Jordan, Joshua called two of his best men to a secret meeting. They were brave and clever soldiers. "I have a secret mission for you," he said.

The two men liked secret missions.

"I want you to spy on the land across the river. Sneak into the city of Jericho. Find out how strong it is. Find out if the people are ready to fight us and how many soldiers they have. See what types of weapons they use. Are they made of bronze or iron? Then come back and tell me. After we cross the River Jordan, we'll attack Jericho."

The men nodded. That afternoon the two spies slipped into the city. It was surrounded by great thick walls. At night the gates were closed tight. Guards patrolled the tops of the walls.

The men walked by a group of soldiers. One of them turned and shouted, "Hey, who are those two strangers?"

"They look like Israelites!"

"Stop! Spies! Those two men are spies, stop them!"

The two could hear the crowd crashing after them. They turned first this way, then that. They dashed through the narrow streets, trying to find a place to hide.

"In here!" someone whispered. The men stopped and looked up. They saw a woman hanging out of a window above them. "In here." She pointed at the door below her. Joshua's spies opened the door and ran in.

91

The Spies Escape

Joshua 2:3-14

The Israelite spies looked around. They saw the woman standing on the other side of the room. "I will hide you," she said. "Follow me."

The Jericho woman led the spies up to the roof of her house. She showed them where to hide. The spies waited until it became dark.

When the king of Jericho had heard about the spies, he ordered his soldiers to search the city. Soon they reached the house where the spies were hiding.

The soldiers entered the woman's house. When they questioned her, she told them, "Yes, they were here, but now they're gone. If you hurry, you can still catch them."

The guards clattered out of the house. They rushed out of the gate just

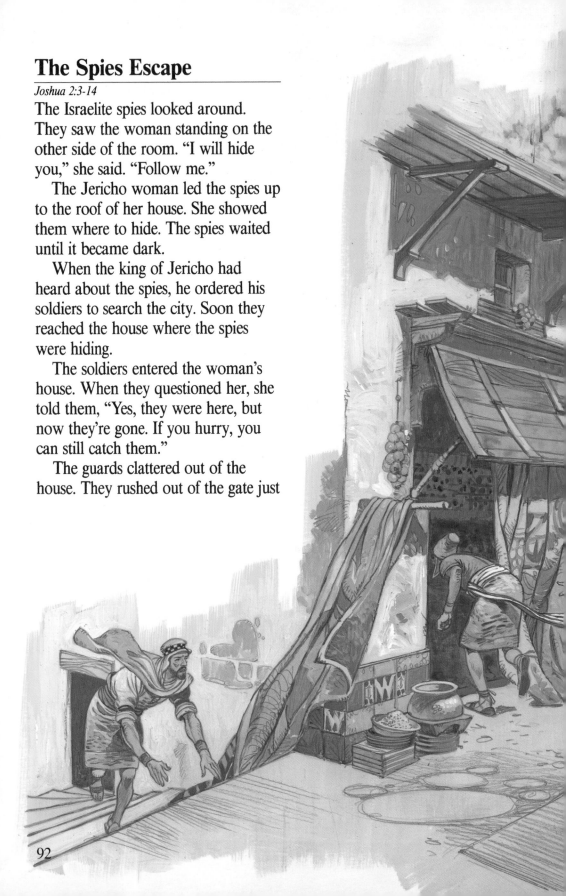

before it closed for the night. Now no matter what, they could not come back in until the next morning.

"Quickly," the woman called to the Israelites. "Quickly, now is your chance. Hurry and leave while the guards are gone."

The two men climbed out of their hiding place. "I know all about you people of Israel," she said. "God is on your side. He blesses whatever you do. All the men in Jericho are scared to fight you.

"If I help you escape, will you remember me and not harm me when you take Jericho?"

"Our lives for yours," the men replied. "Yes, we'll save you if you help us get out of here." The woman nodded. Then she led them up another set of stairs.

Saved by a Red Cord

Joshua 2:15-22

The men climbed the narrow steps until they reached a tiny room. "Here, this is how you will escape," the woman said. She pointed at a small window. That side of the house was actually part of the wall surrounding Jericho. The woman gave the spies some rope. "If you climb out here, you'll land on the outside of the city. Go into the hills. Stay hidden for three days."

The man took the rope from her. "What is your name?"

"I am Rahab."

"Rahab, when Israel attacks, tie this red rope to the window. We'll make sure no one living here gets hurt when we attack Jericho."

The other spy growled, "But if you tell and we are caught, you'll get no mercy from our army."

She nodded. The men opened the window and fastened the red cord to a pillar. Slowly they lowered themselves out of the house. They bounced against the wall with their feet. When they reached the ground, no alarm had sounded. They disappeared into the darkness. Rahab pulled the rope back inside. She knew it was her ticket to safety. If God wanted the people of Israel to capture Jericho, then they surely would.

On the Edge of the Promised Land

Joshua 2:23-3:13

The spies from Israel hid for three days. Once they knew they were safe, they ran back to camp and reported to Joshua.

"It's too good to be true," the men said. "This woman who helped us said all the men in Jericho were afraid of us. The city is ours."

Then the three men bowed their heads and thanked God for helping them. When Joshua finished praying he looked at his men.

"We will invade Jericho a few days from now. Today, though, is the day for which we have waited so long." At first his officers did not understand what he meant. Then a huge grin stretched itself across Joshua's bearded face. "Today is the day the Lord will lead us into the promised land!" The men took up the call and ran to the other leaders. They told the news to everyone in the camp. Soon it spread from one end to the other, "Today is the day!"

The people were so excited. They had hoped for and counted down the days. Forty years of wandering were over!

Crossing the River Jordan

Joshua 3:14-4:24

Joshua ordered the priests to carry the ark across the river. When the priests' toes touched the water, the waves reared back. The water formed a huge wall. A dry path stretched before the priests.

They walked to the middle of the river. Not a drop touched them. They were perfectly dry! Then Joshua called for the people to follow. Family by family, camel by camel, all the people and donkeys and cattle crossed the River Jordan that day. They walked around the priests who held the ark.

It took all day for the people of Israel to pass by the priests. On the other side was their new land. When everyone had crossed the river, Joshua looked down from the hill where he had been watching everything. He remembered the promise of God to his forefather Abraham.

God had said, "I will make you into a great nation. You will number more than all the stars in the sky. This land of Canaan will belong to you."

Joshua told the priests to come on shore. As soon as they were safe, God caused the waves to come crashing down again. After nearly five hundred years, Abraham's children had come home to the promised land.

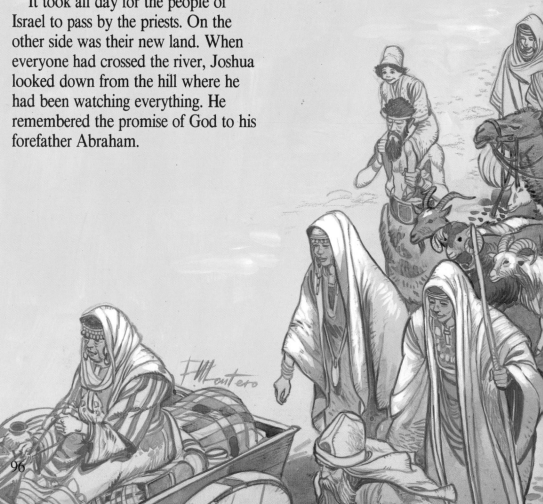

The Battle Won with Trumpets

Joshua 5:13-6:27

Joshua knew he must attack Jericho soon. He prayed for the Lord's help. Then God gave Joshua a very strange plan.

Joshua told his captains, "We will have a parade."

None of Joshua's soldiers had ever fought like that before. A parade was not a battle! But they listened to the plan from God as Joshua told them.

"Yes," they said, "we will try that. We will do what God says."

The next day all the soldiers lined up. It did look like a parade. First the priests carried the ark. Then came Joshua. He led all the soldiers.

The people in the city of Jericho saw the soldiers of Israel coming. They shook with fear. "Oh," they cried,

"this will be a terrible battle. We will all die because God is on their side."

But the Israelites surprised them. They did not attack. Instead, they lined up and walked around the city. They marched around the walls which surrounded the city. And as they marched, the soldiers were very quiet. Joshua had told them not to make a sound. There were no battle cries, no yells or shouts, just hundreds and hundreds of quiet soldiers. The only sound was that of seven priests, playing on their trumpets.

The army of Israel marched around Jericho. Then they went back to their camp and rested.

The next day they did the same thing. For six days, they paraded around Jericho. All the while, they made no sound except for the trumpets.

Then, on the seventh day, Joshua ordered his army to walk around Jericho seven times. After the seventh time, when the trumpets blew, the soldiers let out a great whoop. They yelled as loud as they could.

"Boom! Crash!" No sooner had the soldiers yelled when the very walls of Jericho fell in! God had worked another miracle. The people of Israel poured into the city. Only one family in Jericho lived through that day. That was the woman named Rahab and her family.

The Wise Woman under the Palm Tree

Judges 4:1-16

Many, many years passed. The people of Israel forgot their promises to Moses and to God. They worshipped other gods. So the Lord allowed their enemies King Jabin and his General Sisera to conquer them.

At that time the Lord had sent a woman named Deborah to be a judge over Israel. God had blessed her with wisdom. She loved the Lord God very much. She often told her people to listen to God and obey Him. But most of them just laughed at her.

As a judge, Deborah listened to all the problems of the people. When Deborah held court, she sat underneath a big palm tree. Then all the people stood in line. They waited to talk with her.

One day Deborah sent for Barak, an Israelite soldier. "Barak, you are to take ten thousand men. Lead the way to Mount Tabor. When General Sisera hears you are there, he will bring his chariots and troops. We will fight a great battle and defeat him at the river."

"Well, all right. If you say so, Deborah. But I don't want to fight this battle unless you're there, too."

Deborah smiled at him. "Is your faith in God less than your faith in me?" she asked. "All right. Because you did not trust God, though, He will give the victory to a woman instead of to you."

When the day of the battle came, Barak led his troops. Deborah raised her hands and prayed on the mountaintop. God caused many things to go wrong for Sisera's troops. Before Barak knew it, he was chasing all of Sisera's soldiers into the hills. The people of Israel had won!

Who Will Kill Sisera?

Judges 4:17-22; 5:1-31

When General Sisera saw he had lost the battle, he ran away. He searched for a place to hide. He spotted the home of one of King Jabin's friends. "Ah," he thought, "these people will hide me."

A woman came out to meet him. Her name was Jael. "Come right in," she said. Sisera did not know it, but secretly, Jael hated Sisera and his army. Jael gave him some milk, then she covered him with a blanket.

General Sisera fell sound asleep. Jael tiptoed over to his side. She carried a tent stake and hammer in her hands. Then Jael killed General Sisera.

Meanwhile, Barak was looking for Sisera. As he came to Jael's tent, Jael went out to meet him. She told him what she had done.

Barak brought Jael back to Deborah and to the army. All the people of Israel cheered wildly. They called out, "Who killed Sisera?"

Barak looked at Deborah. The credit for Sisera's death must go to a woman. He held Jael's hand up high so the crowd could see her. "This woman! Jael killed Sisera!"

All the people of Israel cheered Jael. Deborah and Barak told them, though, it was the Lord God who had won the war for them. They even sang a song about God's victory.

Gideon Begins His Work

Judges 6:1-40

It did not take long before the people forgot their promises again. Because they worshipped other gods, God could not make them strong. A terrible tribe called the Midianites conquered them.

God chose a man named Gideon to help His people. He sent an angel who told Gideon he must knock down the altar and statue to other gods. God's people were worshipping this statue on the hill.

Gideon knew the other men in the village could kill him for this. He was afraid to tear down the altar of their gods, but he did it anyway since God had asked him to.

Gideon and ten of his servants climbed the hill. They went to the place where the foreign gods were worshipped. There they smashed the stone altar and the statue to other gods.

Then they very quietly built a new altar. They killed one of the bulls they had brought with them and burned it on the altar. They prayed to God. "Please, Lord, please take care of us."

The next morning when the men of the village found the broken altar, they said, "Who dared to do this? We'll kill him!"

But Joash, Gideon's father, told them, "If your god is really a god, let him punish the culprit. You stay out of it." The men agreed. So Gideon was safe and the altar of the Lord remained.

Soon the Midianites were planning to attack Israel again. Gideon asked God, "Lord, if You are really going to help Israel win, then please show me. I will put this sheepskin on the ground for the night. If it is wet with dew, and the ground around it is dry, then I will know we should go into battle."

And it was so. The next morning the sheepskin was wet, but the ground was dry. Gideon still wanted to be sure. "Lord, forgive me, please. But may I test You yet one more time? Tonight, could You please make the ground wet with dew, but keep the sheepskin dry?"

And it was so. This way Gideon had no doubt at all that he was doing what God wanted.

It Takes Fewer Men to Win the Battle

Judges 7:1-8

Many men followed Gideon. They all wanted to fight against the Midianites. So Gideon led the people to a river. On the other side was the Midianite army.

But the Lord said, "Gideon, there are too many soldiers with you. If you win, the people might become proud. They will think they did it all by themselves. I want to teach them to rely on Me and trust Me. Tell those who are even a little bit afraid to go home." Gideon did so and about half the people went home.

"But there are still too many," God said. "Take them down to the river. Those who kneel and drink will go home. Those who cup the water in their hands and drink will fight the battle."

Gideon did what God told him. And almost all the people knelt to drink. "You," Gideon pointed at the people on their knees, "all of you go on home."

After the people left, Gideon counted how many remained. There were only three hundred men. "God will fight for us," Gideon said.

Listening in the Night

Judges 7:9-15

That same night the Lord told Gideon to cross the river and spy on the Midianites. In the dark night Gideon and his servant crept toward the Midianite camp. There were thousands and thousands of them. There were many more camels than Midianites. The fields were full of camel humps.

God had told Gideon, "When you spy on the Midianites, you will hear something which will help you win the battle."

Inside the camp Gideon hid behind a tent. He heard voices inside.

One Midianite soldier said to another, "I just had the strangest dream. A loaf of bread came tumbling into our camp and turned it upside down."

"I know what that means," the other soldier said. "That's Gideon and his Israelite army. They will beat our army tomorrow because the one, true God is leading them."

Gideon thought to himself, "Even the Midianites are scared of me. They know God is on our side."

Trumpets and Torches

Judges 7:15-8:21

Gideon thought to himself, "If the enemy soldiers are this scared, then we've almost won." Gideon bowed his head. He thanked God.

Gideon hurried back to the Israelite camp. He woke up his soldiers and told them what he had heard. "We've practically won already. All we have

104

to do is attack now, and take them by surprise. If we make as much noise as possible, they will think there are more than three hundred of us. Tonight, men, you will see how great the Lord is!" The soldiers waved their spears in the air and cheered.

"Yes," Gideon said, "just like that. When I give the sign, once we're near the Midianites, cheer as loud as you can. Yell out, 'For God and for Gideon!' That will scare them!"

Gideon divided the men into three groups. He sent them out to surround the enemy camp. All was quiet. Not even the camels knew Gideon's troops were there.

Then, suddenly, Gideon gave the signal. His men blew their trumpets. They shouted, broke the jars that

had shielded their lights, and blew their trumpets. It made a terrific noise! The Midianites thought a mighty army had come to attack them. They woke up with a start. They ran away as fast as they could. Because the noise came from all around them, though, they did not even know which way to run. It was a mighty victory for Gideon.

Gideon and his men lit their torches. They drove off every single Midianite. Only a few got away. But even those few were not safe. Gideon and his men chased these last enemy soldiers a long, long way.

"The Lord has helped us win today," Gideon told the people of Israel. All the people bowed their heads and gave thanks to God.

Fighting with a Lion

Judges 13:1-14:7

Many, many years later God's people were still worshipping false gods. Now their enemy was the Philistine tribe. At that time there lived a couple with a very special son. His name was Samson.

Samson's parents had never cut Samson's hair. This was a sign that he belonged to God. They knew God had a special plan for Samson.

As Samson grew older, the Lord sent His Holy Spirit to make Samson super strong. God did this whenever He wanted to teach Samson a special lesson.

Samson had a Philistine girlfriend. He wanted to marry her. So Samson and his parents went to the girl's village to plan the wedding.

On the way there, Samson followed his parents. They were a few hours ahead of him. At one point, he walked through a field and heard a strange sound.

"What is that?" he wondered.

Then suddenly, from out of nowhere, a great big lion came running at him. "Raaaaahh!" The lion's long teeth shone. He opened his mouth and roared.

Samson had no weapons at all. But the Spirit of the Lord came upon him. He became stronger than the strongest man. He was super strong. When the lion was on him, Samson threw him off and killed him!

106

Samson Tells a Riddle

Judges 14:8-15:20

Later, a few days before the wedding, Samson passed by the place where he had killed the lion. There was a swarm of bees making honey. He went over to the lion and tasted the honey. It was very sweet.

That night Samson was talking with some of the men in his girlfriend's village. Samson said, "I know a good riddle. Does anyone want to place a bet with me?"

"Sure, I will."

"Yes," all the men agreed. Samson bet them thirty pieces of linen and thirty changes of clothes. They had to answer the riddle before the eighth day after the wedding. The men agreed.

Samson said, "This is the riddle: Out of the eater came something to eat. Out of the strong came something sweet."

No one knew the answer. The wedding took place and four days of parties passed. The thirty Philistines could not figure out the answer to the riddle. So they ordered Samson's wife, "Get Samson to tell you the riddle's answer. If you don't, we'll burn down

108

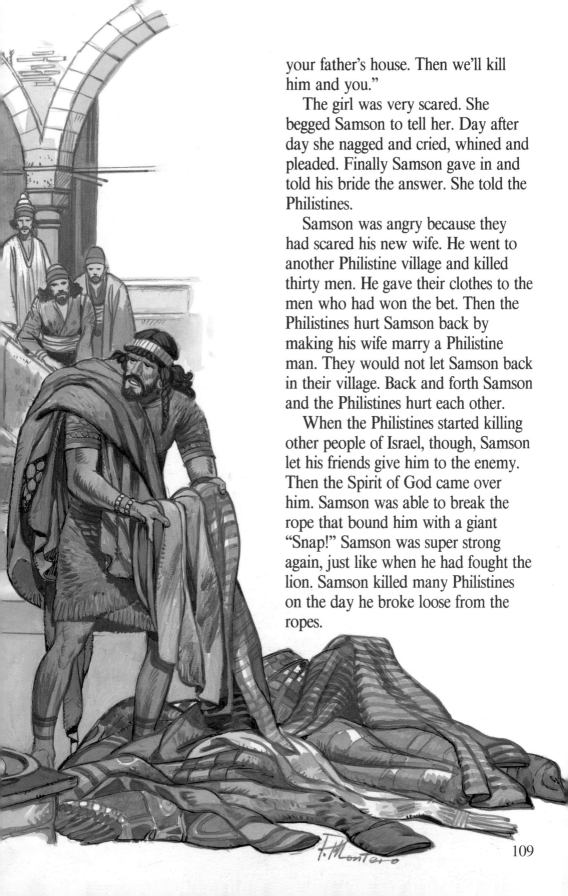

your father's house. Then we'll kill him and you."

The girl was very scared. She begged Samson to tell her. Day after day she nagged and cried, whined and pleaded. Finally Samson gave in and told his bride the answer. She told the Philistines.

Samson was angry because they had scared his new wife. He went to another Philistine village and killed thirty men. He gave their clothes to the men who had won the bet. Then the Philistines hurt Samson back by making his wife marry a Philistine man. They would not let Samson back in their village. Back and forth Samson and the Philistines hurt each other.

When the Philistines started killing other people of Israel, though, Samson let his friends give him to the enemy. Then the Spirit of God came over him. Samson was able to break the rope that bound him with a giant "Snap!" Samson was super strong again, just like when he had fought the lion. Samson killed many Philistines on the day he broke loose from the ropes.

Samson and Delilah

Judges 16:1-20

For twenty years Samson's enemies left him alone. He became a judge over Israel. Samson taught the people how to follow God's laws. Throughout that time, the Spirit of God made Samson very strong. He was famous for his muscles. With the Lord's help, Samson could do anything.

The Philistines still wanted to capture Samson. One day, after so many years, Samson fell in love again. The woman he loved was called Delilah. She was a bad woman. She made a deal with the Philistines. She would trick Samson and hand him over to his enemies. Then they would give her very many silver pieces.

Over and over again, she nagged Samson. "Why are you so strong? What is your secret?"

Samson did not like being nagged. It reminded him of how he had lost

his wife. "Please, please, please, Samson. Tell me your secret!" Delilah asked Samson morning, noon and night. She would not give up. She wanted the silver pieces very much.

Finally, Samson could not stand it any longer. "All right, woman!" he bellowed. "I've had enough! The secret of my strength is the Lord. He makes me strong as long as my hair is uncut. Ever since I was a baby my parents knew God had a plan for me."

That night Delilah called the Philistines again. She made Samson sleep on her lap. She made sure he would not wake up as the Philistines crept in. A man cut his hair, and when Samson did wake up, it was already too late. Samson was too weak to fight the Philistines. They took Samson prisoner and paid Delilah her money.

The Strongest Man Wins

Judges 16:21-31

When the Philistines dragged Samson away, they were very happy. After twenty years, they had finally captured Samson. "All we had to do was cut your hair! Now you're as weak as a baby!"

The Philistines were very mean. They took out Samson's eyes so that he became blind. Then they threw him into prison.

Poor Samson. He had no hope of escaping. After some time his hair started growing back again. Little by little, he felt the Lord returning his strength. He would never see again. He prayed he might someday be able to pay back the Philistines for all they had done to him.

"Lord," he cried out, "give me back my strength."

As the months passed, Samson became stronger and stronger. One day, the Philistines were having a huge party in a big hall. There were over three thousand people there.

"Let's have Samson come to the party, too," they said.

"Yes, we can laugh at him."

The prison guard brought Samson to them. As Samson entered the hall, he heard them making fun of him. Samson asked the boy who led him to let him feel the pillars in the middle of the hall. These pillars held the big house up.

When Samson felt the rough stone beneath his fingers, he shouted, "Lord God Almighty, please give me back my strength! Just this one last time, let me hurt the Philistines. Please Lord, help me set Your people free!"

The Lord heard Samson. His Holy Spirit flooded Samson with strength. With a mighty heave, Samson pushed the pillars. He pushed and heaved and shoved and suddenly, with a mighty crash, the stones all fell in on one another!

"Let me die with the Philistines!" Samson shouted. And he bent with all his might so that the house fell down.

113

A Bad Time

Ruth 1:1-13

There once was a woman named Naomi. She was one of the few people who still liked to pray to God. When she married, she moved away from her home. She had two sons whom she loved very much. Then her husband died.

As Naomi raised her boys, she taught them about the Lord. When they were grown up, her sons married. The girls they married belonged to the Moabite tribe. These had been enemies of Israel for many years. This did not seem to matter to Naomi, though. She loved these girls as if they were her own daughters.

Then the two sons died. Naomi and the two young wives were left alone. Oh, it was a very sad time for the three women! The wives were called Orpah and Ruth. They lived with Naomi and helped in any way they could. But there was not much food in the land. The three women could not find enough to eat.

"My daughters," Naomi said. "I have heard there is food in the land where I grew up. That is far away from here. My people were one of the tribes of Israel. I'll go there now, but it would be better for you to go back to your own parents. They'll take care of you. Maybe you'll even find husbands again."

The young women said, "No. We want to stay with you."

But Naomi shook her head. "What will you do? I'm too old to find another husband. Don't be silly. Go back home." Naomi loved her daughters-in-law and wanted them to stay. But she also wanted to do what was best for them.

A Woman of Loyalty

Ruth 1:14-22

Orpah came up to Naomi. She said, "I will do what you wish. I will go back to my parents." The old woman

hugged her. They held each other and cried. They knew they would never see each other again. Orpah gathered her things and left.

But Ruth would not leave. She put a hand on Naomi's shoulder. She said she would stay, no matter what. In her heart Naomi was glad Ruth wanted to stay. Naomi knew she would become an old beggar woman, with no one to help her. She wanted what was best for Ruth, though. "You must go, too, Ruth."

was where Naomi had grown up. When they arrived, all the old people remembered Naomi. "Is it really you?" they asked.

"Naomi, you've come back to us! It's so nice to see you again."

Old friends hugged her and the word soon spread, "Naomi has come back home! She's brought her daughter-in-law with her."

Ruth Goes to Work

Ruth 2:1-22

Naomi felt glad to be back home. She knew, though, that she and Ruth still must find a way to feed themselves. The next morning Ruth told Naomi, "We have no more food. It's time for me to find work. The barley harvest has started. I'll go into the fields and see if there's any barley left over. Whatever I find I'll bring home."

Naomi nodded. "Go, my daughter." She prayed Ruth would find some grain to eat.

It was a very special thing for Ruth to go out alone and look for work in that strange country. It showed how much she really trusted God to help her.

Ruth went to a field owned by a rich man called Boaz. Boaz happened to be from the same family as Naomi. When Boaz saw Ruth, he called her to him.

"Please, sir," Ruth said. "Please may I pick up any barley which your servants leave behind?"

Ruth begged Naomi, "No, you're my mother now. Please, Naomi, let me go with you. I'll go where you go. Your people will be my people and your God, my God." Ruth knew about the one, true God. Her husband had taught her about God and she trusted Him. "Please, Naomi," Ruth begged. "I never want to be far away from you. God will take care of us."

Naomi finally agreed. The two women set off for Bethlehem. That

"Of course, of course," Boaz said. "I've heard how good you have been to your mother-in-law. I'll help you any way I can." So Boaz ordered his servants to share their food with her.

That day Ruth worked hard and gathered a full basket of barley. That was more than enough for her and Naomi. She brought the basket home that evening, together with the food left over from lunch.

"Ruth!" Naomi's eyes nearly popped out of her head. "Ruth, where on earth did you find so much food?"

"Oh Naomi, I met a man who was so kind and good. His name is Boaz and he helped me. He said I can come and gather leftover grain in his fields whenever I want to."

Then, for the first time in many, many months, Naomi smiled. She said, "Oh, Ruth. Boaz is a member of my family. If Boaz is taking care of us, then the Lord has finally started blessing us again."

The two women sat down to eat. They thanked God for taking such good care of them. They prayed, too, that God would be good to Boaz because he had been so good to them.

117

The Great-grandmother of a King

Ruth 2:23-4:22

For the rest of the barley harvest, Ruth worked hard in Boaz's fields. She always came home with more food than she needed.

Near the end of the harvest Naomi said to Ruth, "You're so young and pretty. Why don't we see if you can marry Boaz?" When Ruth agreed, Naomi said she had a plan.

That night Naomi sent Ruth off to see Boaz. Boaz was sleeping under the stars. Ruth crept up to him and lay down at his feet. In the middle of the night he woke up with a start.

"Who's there, sleeping by my feet?" he whispered in the dark.

"It's me, Ruth. I've come to ask if

you would please think about maybe taking me as your wife. You're part of Naomi's family, after all. I need to have a husband. Boaz, you've always been so good to me."

Boaz sat up. "My dear, you are so lovely. Any man would be honoured to make you his wife. You're very special to come and ask me like this. Yes, will you marry me?"

Ruth nodded and Boaz leaned over to kiss her. Boaz and Ruth smiled at each other. "Let me talk to the village leaders. We'll get married as soon as possible," Boaz said. He squeezed Ruth's hand. Then he kissed Ruth again and sent her home.

When Ruth saw Naomi, she told her the good news. The next day they told all their friends. When it came time for the wedding, it was a great party. All of Bethlehem was there.

As the years went by, Boaz and Ruth grew to love each other very much. The Lord blessed them with a little boy. Ruth and Boaz had Naomi move in with them. That way she could help take care of her little grandson, Obed.

Obed grew up to be a good man. He loved God and followed His laws. Many, many years later, David, the great king of Israel, was born into Obed's family. So Ruth and Boaz, because of their loyalty and kindness, were blessed by God. They became the great-grandparents of a mighty king!

Waiting for a Baby

1 Samuel 1:1-5

Long after Ruth's son Obed was born, the people of Israel were still choosing to forget God. Most people did not even try to pray.

At this time there lived a man named Elkanah. Elkanah had two wives. One had children and the other had none. Elkanah's wife who had no children was called Hannah. She had long black hair and dark eyes which lit up when she smiled. Elkanah loved Hannah very much.

The years went by, and Hannah still did not have any children. Elkanah loved Hannah even more than he loved his other wife. She was called Peninnah. Peninnah had given Elkanah many sons and daughters. She was not as gentle and good as Hannah.

Peninnah knew Elkanah loved Hannah more than her. This made Peninnah very jealous. Every chance she had, she teased Hannah and made fun of her. She often told Hannah she was a useless wife since she could not give Elkanah even one child.

Elkanah was one of the few people at that time who tried to follow the Lord. Once a year he took the whole family to Shiloh. There the ark containing the Ten Commandments was kept in a holy tent. A priest took care of the ark there.

Each year, after Elkanah finished worshipping God at Shiloh, he held a big party for his family. Hannah was there, together with Peninnah and all her children.

Every year at the feast in Shiloh, Elkanah gave Hannah twice as much meat as Peninnah. He felt so badly about Hannah not having any little children. He thought it was the least he could do. Elkanah hoped the extra meat might bring back Hannah's special smile. He remembered that smile well, but hardly saw it at all anymore.

121

Peninnah Hurts Hannah

1 Samuel 1:6-8

Every year at the feast in Shiloh, Peninnah watched Elkanah give Hannah more meat than anyone else. And each year she made sure she said something cruel to Hannah.

Year after year, Peninnah would lean across the table and whisper to Hannah, "Meat is better than nothing, I suppose. You're nobody special. Elkanah just feels sorry for you because you have no children."

Each year Peninnah's insults became worse. Finally one year, Peninnah's teasing was crueller than ever. "You're getting old, Hannah. Look, my eldest is nearly a grown man now. And you have no one. What will you do when you're no longer pretty? Then Elkanah will stop giving you extra meat. You won't even have one son to show for your youth."

Hannah could not take it anymore. She covered her ears and burst into tears. She wanted a baby so badly. "Why, oh why don't I have a child?" she cried out in her heart.

Elkanah saw his favourite wife crying. He guessed what Peninnah had said. He told Hannah, "Hannah, don't be upset about not having a child. That's all right, it doesn't matter."

But it was not all right and it did matter. Hannah ran away from the table.

123

A Prayer from the Heart

1 Samuel 1:9-18

Hannah walked to the tent where the priest made offerings to God. She did not know what to do. She knelt down and put her face in her hands. Her lips moved as she prayed. The tears streamed down her face.

"Oh Lord," she prayed quietly. "I want a baby so badly. Please, God, if You would give me a little child, I would give him back to You. I would bring it here to be raised by Your priest. The child would be Yours."

As Hannah prayed, Eli the priest watched her. He saw her lips moving. He heard no sound. Hannah's eyes were red from crying.

In those days, there were not many people of Israel who went to Eli's tent to pray. Those who did, prayed out loud. Some who came to Shiloh had come just to eat and drink. The priest saw Hannah's red eyes and her lips which moved. He thought she had had too much wine to drink.

"You there!" he yelled at her. "You shouldn't come here if you're drunk."

"No, my lord," Hannah gasped. "I'm not one of those drunken people who stumble in here during the feast! I'm just very, very sad."

As Eli came closer to Hannah, he saw that she spoke the truth. "Go in peace. I hope God gives you what you've asked for."

Hannah bowed her head. "Thank you for your blessing sir." As Hannah walked away, she felt the weight of worry and shame lift off her heart. Whether or not she ever did get a baby was up to the Lord. She knew now whatever He decided would be the best for her and Elkanah.

Baby Samuel

1 Samuel 1:19-25

Hannah went home with Elkanah. A few months later she found out she was going to have a baby. Oh, that was a happy day for Hannah! She thanked God over and over again.

Nearly a year later, Hannah gave birth to a lovely baby boy. She named him Samuel, which meant "Heard of God." Hannah said, "because I asked the Lord for him and He heard."

Now when Peninnah teased Hannah, it did not hurt at all. If Peninnah said, "Hannah, I have many more sons than you," Hannah did not mind.

"Yes, but my Samuel is worth ten sons," Hannah answered.

For the next three years Hannah took care of Samuel. She played with him and prayed with him. She taught him how to count. She sang songs and danced with him. They often laughed together.

After Samuel turned three, Hannah knew the time had come for her to bring him back to Eli. Samuel had been a gift from God. She had trusted God to decide whether or not she should have a baby. Now she was trusting God to take care of her son.

Hannah Leaves Samuel with Eli

1 Samuel 1:26-2:11

Hannah held Samuel's hand. They stood at the door of the tent in Shiloh where the Lord was worshipped. "Eli!" Hannah called out. When the old man appeared, Hannah said, "Remember me? I'm the woman whose prayers you blessed three years ago. I was praying for a baby then. Look how the Lord has answered my prayers." She smiled down at Samuel.

Samuel knew he was a special boy. He belonged to God. He knew the priest Eli would now take care of him. Samuel was not afraid. His mother had told him God would take care of him, no matter where he was. Samuel trusted her and he trusted the Lord. Besides, she would visit him each year when the family came to Shiloh.

Samuel knew he was a big boy. He did not cry. He just looked at Eli, then back at his mother. He waited for her to take her hand out of his. "Then I might cry," he thought.

Hannah told Eli about her promise to God. Eli nodded. He stooped down and stretched out his arms toward the boy. Samuel looked at the kind eyes of old Eli, the priest. He knew he was safe.

Becoming a Priest

1 Samuel 2:18-21; 3:1

Little Samuel was happy living with Eli the priest. Eli was like a father to Samuel. This was just as well since Eli's own sons were greedy and selfish. They did not care about God, but Samuel did.

Every year Hannah and Elkanah brought Samuel a new robe. Whenever Samuel felt a little homesick, he put on his robe and thought about his mother hugging him.

Samuel helped Eli in the temple. His job was to keep all the lamps lit. He learned about the different types of offerings Eli made to God. Samuel also learned that praying was just like talking to God. Sometimes, though, he wondered why he did not hear God answer back.

Samuel Hears God's Voice

1 Samuel 3:2-18

One night Samuel was asleep when he heard a Voice calling his name, "Samuel."

"Here I am," Samuel said. He ran to Eli. "Yes, Eli. Did you call me? What did you want, sir?" Samuel asked.

The old man sat up in bed and scratched his beard. "I didn't call you," he said. "Go back to sleep. It's the middle of the night."

Samuel did as he was told. No sooner was he asleep when he heard again, "Samuel!" Samuel woke up and ran to Eli.

"Yes, Eli," the boy said.

"No, my son, I didn't call you," Eli said again.

Later that night, Samuel heard for a third time the Voice saying, "Samuel!" Samuel had never heard the voice of God before. He still thought it was Eli who called him.

Once again he ran to Eli. And this time Eli knew Samuel must have heard the Lord's voice. It had been a long, long time since God had spoken to any of the people of Israel. Eli told Samuel, "The Lord God has been

128

calling you! Answer Him next time by saying, 'Yes, Lord, I am listening.'"

The boy did as he was told. The next time the Lord spoke to Samuel, He said, "I have seen the bad things Eli's sons have been doing. From now on I will speak through you, Samuel."

The next morning Samuel told Eli everything the Lord had said. This was the first of many times God spoke to Samuel.

The Lost Donkeys

1 Samuel 8:1-9:25

Samuel grew up to become a great prophet. He told the people what God wanted. There came a time, though, when the people were telling God what they wanted. They wanted a king.

"No, you should make God your King," Samuel said.

But the people would not listen.

"All right," Samuel said. "You will get your king. Now go back home."

At this time there was a very handsome man from the smallest tribe of Israel. His name was Saul. Saul's father had lost some donkeys and sent his son to go out looking for them.

Saul and his servant searched high and low for the donkeys. They could not find them. Saul was gone many, many days. Finally Saul wanted to go back home. His servant said, "There's a man of God living near here. He's very wise. Maybe we should ask him if he knows where the donkeys are."

The two men headed for Samuel's house. It just so happened that God had told Samuel the day before, "A stranger will visit you tomorrow. He is the one who will become king over My people."

Samuel spent all that day watching for the stranger. When Saul saw him, standing in the gateway, he asked, "Do you know where the holy man of God is?"

"I am he," Samuel said. "And the Lord has already told me about you. Your donkeys are safe. Come with me to the top of that hill." Samuel pointed. "There's a banquet going on there. You may eat at the head of the table. Some day you will become a very important man."

Saul could hardly believe what he was hearing as he followed Samuel up the hill.

130

The Big Secret

1 Samuel 9:26-10:8

After the banquet, Saul spent the night at Samuel's house. They slept on Samuel's roof since it was so hot. The next morning Samuel told Saul it was time for him to go home.

As the two men walked toward the edge of town, Samuel stopped. He turned to Saul and poured oil over his head. This meant Saul was a special man in the eyes of God. "The Lord has chosen you to lead His people and rule over them as king."

Saul bowed his head. "How can this be!" he wondered.

All that had happened seemed so big and impossible. How could Samuel know all this? The answer, very simply, was God had told him.

"Saul, when you leave here today, you'll meet two men who will say, 'The donkeys which you've been looking for have been found.' Now return to your father, before he starts to worry."

Saul Becomes King

1 Samuel 10:9-27

As Saul turned to leave Samuel, God did a very special thing. He changed his heart. Now when Saul saw all the things Samuel had predicted would happen, he knew it was because God had made it happen.

Later that day Saul did find out about the donkeys, exactly as Samuel had said he would.

Soon after this Samuel called the people together. "Do you still want a king?"

The people yelled, "Yes, we want a king!"

"All right, God will choose a king for you," Samuel said. Then Samuel threw lots, which were a type of dice. Through the lots God chose the tribe of Benjamin. One by one, Samuel went through the families of Benjamin. God showed He wanted the Matri family. This was Saul's family.

Then Samuel went through each man in that family until God chose Saul. He asked, "Where is this man?"

"Who is Saul?" The people all looked around. "Where is he?"

Samuel asked the Lord. He told them Saul was hiding among the bags and baskets.

The people ran and found Saul. They brought him before Samuel. "See how tall he is," Samuel said. "This is your king!"

The people cheered, "Long live the king!"

Samuel told the people about the rules they would have to follow if they had a king. Then he wrote them down on a scroll.

As long as Saul followed God's rules, the Lord would bless him.

God Chooses a New King

1 Samuel 15:9-16:13

At first Saul tried to be a good king.
He ruled the way God wanted him to.
As time went by, Saul became greedy.
God did not like it when Saul only
cared about himself. So God asked
Samuel to go and find the next king.

"I want you to take oil to
Bethlehem. Ask to see the sons of
Jesse. There I will show you the next
king."

When Samuel arrived in Bethlehem,
he sent for Jesse's sons. The eldest was
very handsome.

But the Lord said, "I am God. I do
not measure people by their looks. I
look at a person's heart and see what
you do not see."

When all seven sons had walked
past Samuel, he turned to Jesse. "The
Lord has not chosen any of these. Do
you have any other sons?"

"Well," Jesse said, "there is one
more. But he's the youngest. He's out
looking after the sheep." So Jesse's
youngest son David was called for.

The boy had large brown eyes and
was darkly tanned. His smile seemed
to light the very room. He was
handsome and strong.

The Lord said, "This is the one."
Samuel took the oil and poured it over
David's head. This meant David had
been chosen to be the king.

Then Samuel went back home. God
had chosen His next king, but it was

not time to tell all the people about it.
Not yet.

David Cares for Saul

1 Samuel 16:14-23

David went back to watching over the
sheep in the pastures. Whenever a lion
or wolf threatened his sheep, David
shot them with his sling. During the
long days in the meadows, David
often played his harp and sang songs
of praise to the Lord.

As David grew closer to God, Saul
grew further and further away. God's
Spirit left Saul. Saul's mind grew dark
and tortured. Saul could not sleep. He
was always sad and tense. He never
felt like eating. Sometimes his mind
played tricks on him. He imagined
things which were not there. Often he
felt as if he were two different people,
locked into the same body.

Saul's servants said he must find
someone who could calm him.
"Where is such a man?" Saul asked.

"I've heard about a son of Jesse. He
plays lovely music, is brave, doesn't
talk too much and is handsome," a
servant said. "Not only that, but the
Lord is with him."

Saul sent for David. Jesse sent his
son away, together with a donkey
loaded with gifts of bread and wine for
King Saul.

When David arrived, he played his
harp for the king. This helped Saul
very much.

Even David's brothers were too afraid to fight Goliath.

Goliath's Insults

1 Samuel 17:20-30

For over a month Goliath threatened the Israelite army. At this time, Jesse happened to ask David if he would bring supplies to his brothers. David was glad to go.

When David reached the camp, he looked everywhere for his brothers. Just then, a great cry went up from the Israelite soldiers.

"Run for your lives! It's the giant!"

Goliath bellowed, "Ha! I knew it, you Israelites are all just an army of cowards. I dare Israel to prove me wrong. Your God is weak! He can't help you!"

Goliath had said a terrible, terrible thing. He had said God was weak. When David heard Goliath's insults, he grew very angry. He tried to find out more from the frightened soldiers around him. He heard about the reward. Saul had offered riches and his daughter in marriage to any man who would fight Goliath.

David the Giant-Killer

1 Samuel 17:31-54

David went to Saul. He told him, "Let me fight this Goliath. I don't want God's people to look like cowards."

Saul said, "You can't fight him. You're just a boy."

The Giant

1 Samuel 17:1-19

During the next few years David often visited the palace and played his harp for Saul. Sometimes Saul had to leave and fight wars against the Philistines. Then David would go home to his father.

Among Saul's soldiers were three of David's elder brothers. Jesse often told David to bring grain and bread and cheese to his brothers. That way he could hear how his sons were doing.

During one battle, Saul and his soldiers had a big problem. No fighting had started yet because of a Philistine soldier named Goliath. Goliath was a very, very, very tall man. To most of the Israelites, he looked just like a giant. Goliath the giant had challenged the Israelites.

"If any of you want to fight me, then I dare you to try. If I win, you will all become our slaves. If your man wins, then we have to serve you."

All Saul's men took one look at Goliath and shivered in fear. "How can we fight a giant like that?" they whispered. No one dared to fight him.

David stuck his chin out. "I've saved my sheep from lions and bears."

Finally Saul agreed. He gave David his armour and weapons. They were too big. Since David was not used to wearing such heavy armour, he threw it off. "I will meet Goliath dressed as a shepherd."

Then David chose five smooth stones from a nearby brook. It was time to fight the giant.

When Goliath saw him, he roared, "What an insult! You dare to send a

little boy to fight the great Goliath?"

But David told him, "You might have a sword and spear. My weapon is the name of the Lord God Almighty. He is the God of our army, the very One you made fun of.

"Today God will help me strike you down and take off your head! Then the whole world will know it's not a sword which wins battles, but the power of the Lord!"

Goliath moved closer to attack David. Suddenly, David darted toward Goliath. He fitted his sling with a stone. David swung it around and around his head, then let it fly.

It whirred through the air faster than it took Goliath to raise his spear. Too late, the stone bored a hole right into Goliath's head! The great giant fell with a mighty thud, onto the ground.

David took Goliath's big, heavy sword. He killed him and cut his head off. The Philistines could not believe their eyes. They turned and ran. The men of Israel and Judah did not let them get away. A great battle was won that day, because David trusted in God's power.

139

King Saul Is Jealous

1 Samuel 17:55-58; 18:5-30

When David killed Goliath, Saul made David a general. He sent him out to fight many battles. Every time David returned from a war, he became more and more of a hero.

One time, when David came back from killing many Philistines, a group of Israelite women gathered around him and Saul. They sang, "Saul has killed his thousands and David his tens of thousands."

This made Saul very angry and jealous. He thought to himself, "David's already more popular than I am. Soon he may even try to take my kingdom away." From that day on, Saul was jealous of David.

Saul even tried to get David killed by sending him on dangerous missions. David just became more of a hero. One time, David was off fighting the Philistines. Saul's daughter, Michal, prayed he might return alive. She loved David very much. Because God was with David he did everything well. This time was no different.

When he came back with the proof of his killing, Saul grew even more afraid of David. David had the Lord with him, and Saul did not. The people loved David. They cheered whenever he passed through the city. David and Michal were married. Now David had the love of Saul's daughter to make him even stronger.

Friends for Life

1 Samuel 18:1-4; 19:1-7

Just after David killed Goliath, Saul brought David back to his palace. That was where David first met Jonathan. Jonathan was Saul's son and Michal's brother.

On that day, David had been talking with Saul. David heard someone behind him. He turned, and saw Jonathan. The two young men had stared at each other.

In that split second, the soul of Jonathan was knit to the soul of David. Jonathan knew he had found a best friend for life. From that moment on, Jonathan loved David as himself. The two young men promised to be best friends for ever and ever. Jonathan gave his robe, sword, bow and belt to David.

Years later, Saul told Jonathan and his servants to kill David.

But Jonathan was more than a brother to David. He ran to him and said, "My father wants to kill you! Please, be very, very careful in the morning. You must hide. Then I will talk to my father about you."

Jonathan spent the next morning with his father. He talked about how good David was and how wrong Saul was to try and have him killed.

Finally, Saul promised not to hurt David. David came back to the palace.

But Saul did not keep his promise. Soon he became angry all over again.

Jonathan Saves David's Life

1 Samuel 19:9-20:42; Psalm 59

Saul could not be trusted. One evening, David was playing his harp for Saul. Suddenly, Saul sprang out of his chair and grabbed his spear! He flung it with all his might at David. David ran from the room as fast as he could. He just barely got away.

That night David's wife Michal helped him escape from Saul's soldiers. David made his way to Samuel's home. He told him everything that had happened. Then David circled back and found Jonathan.

"What have I done?" he cried. Jonathan and David thought up a plan. They agreed on a signal.

Jonathan would talk with Saul about David. Afterwards Jonathan would go into the field and practice shooting arrows. If Saul really did want to hunt down David and kill him, Jonathan would shout at the boy chasing his arrows, "Look, the arrows are beyond you." That would be David's signal.

Jonathan walked with David out to the field where they would soon meet again. The two young men felt very close. Jonathan cried out to God, "Be our Witness! If my father wants to hurt David and I don't warn him, let the Lord punish me. Let my children and his be best of friends for ever, even after the Lord destroys all of David's enemies!" Then David hid in the field. Jonathan went back to wait for his

142

father.

Two days later, Jonathan asked Saul about David. His father flew into a rage. Saul even threw his spear at Jonathan, but missed.

The next morning, Jonathan ran to the field with his bow and arrow. He shot an arrow and told the boy who was chasing it, "Look, the arrows are beyond you. Go quickly!" Then he sent the boy home. David came out of hiding.

David fell down on the ground at Jonathan's feet. The two friends were so sad they hugged and cried. Both young men knew it would be a long time before they could see each other again.

144

Alone in a Cave

1 Samuel 24:1-22; Psalm 57

Saul hunted David as if he were an animal. He knew that David was hiding in a place where there were many caves. Saul and his soldiers started searching these hillsides.

At some point, when Saul was alone, he looked around for a place where he could relieve himself. He saw a nearby cave and went inside. There was no way he could have known, but David was hiding inside that same cave!

"Look David," his men whispered to him. "God has blessed you again. Now is your chance to kill Saul!"

David shook his head. He told them, "No one kills God's choice of king!"

Then he crawled down the cave, toward Saul. Very quietly, he cut a corner off Saul's robe. Then he crept back to his hiding place. The moment he was back with his men, David felt very sorry for what he had done. He had not wanted to harm Saul. "I should never even have cut off this corner of his robe."

So Saul got up and left the cave. Once he was outside, though, David came running after him. He fell on the ground. "My lord the king!" he called out. Saul swirled around in surprise. David held up the cloth. "Look, I cut off this corner of your robe. God gave you into my hands while you were in the cave. But I didn't hurt you! I even kept my own men from hurting you. Now will you believe I'm not your enemy? Why do you chase me like this? I've done nothing wrong!"

Saul saw that David could have killed him if he had wanted to. "A man does not let his enemy escape as easily as you have. I believe you, David."

Saul left David and his men in peace . . . for a little while, at least. Soon, though, Saul went back on his promise.

145

146

Everything Is Lost

1 Samuel 29:1-30:31

The fierce Philistines were going to attack Israel. Among the leaders was King Achish of Gath. This king had been protecting David while he ran away from Saul. Achish asked David and his men to march with him. He wanted David to fight against his own people, the Israelites.

When the Philistine generals heard this, they said, "No, we don't want David with us during this battle. What if he decides to change sides?"

So Achish sent David and his men back to their families. David went home to Ziklag. That is where he had been living for over a year. In Ziklag, he made a terrible discovery.

The town was in flames! While David and his men had been gone, the Amalekites had raided the area! All their families had been taken prisoner!

David rallied his men. Six hundred followed him. Two hundred, who were too tired, remained behind.

All that day they tracked the Amalekites. Just as it grew dark, David and his men attacked. They fought long and hard through the night and into the next day. Women and children ran in all directions. Finally, David and his men won the battle. Only four hundred Amalekites escaped alive. And that only happened because they had camels.

David Loses Saul and Jonathan

1 Samuel 31:1-13; 2 Samuel 1:1-27; 1 Chronicles 10:1-14

David returned home to Ziklag. There he heard news of the great battle between Saul's Israelites and the Philistines. This was the battle the Philistine generals had not allowed David to join in.

"It was a terrible battle," the messenger told David. "The Philistines pressed hard after Saul and his sons. They killed his three sons, including Jonathan...."

David cried out, "Oh, no! Not my brother Jonathan!"

The messenger went on. "The king was surrounded. He had no choice. Saul fell on his own sword, killing himself."

At this, David and his men moaned and wept. They did not eat for the whole day. The king anointed by God was dead! It was a dark day for Israel!

147

David Is Crowned

2 Samuel 5:1-10, 13-25; 1 Chronicles 14:1-17

Now that Saul's sons were dead, the tribes of Israel came to David. "We're all part of the same family. Even while Saul was king, you were our leader. We've heard how the Lord has chosen you. We want you to be our king!"

When David became king he chose Jerusalem as his city. At that time Jerusalem was just a small village. Even so, it was well protected and would be very hard to capture.

The Jebusites, who lived in Jerusalem, laughed at David. "Ha! You couldn't even fight the blind and crippled of Jerusalem, let alone us!" But David had the blessing of God. When he and his men captured Jerusalem, they made it the royal city of Israel and Judah.

When the Philistines heard that David was king, they called all their troops together so they could attack him. But David asked the Lord what he should do. God told him, "Do not attack right away, but circle around behind them. When you hear the sound of marching in the tops of the trees, move quickly. That will mean the Lord has gone in front of you to strike down the enemy army."

It happened just that way. David defeated the Philistines everywhere he went.

David was thirty years old when he became king of Judah. He was one of the greatest kings the Jewish people ever had. He reigned over both Israel and Judah for forty years in all.

The Ark of God Arrives in Jerusalem

2 Samuel 6:12-23; 1 Chronicles 15:1-16:43

Jerusalem became David's royal city. He decided to bring the Ark of God to Jerusalem. David had his priests carry the ark on poles. This was the way God had told Moses the ark should be carried.

When the ark arrived in Jerusalem, the priests put it into a special tent David had made.

Then there was great feasting and dancing. Oh, what a party! David had put together a choir and orchestra. They played beautiful music for God.

The people praised and thanked God for all the good things He had done for them. They remembered what God had said to Abraham, Isaac and Jacob. They told the stories of how God rescued them from the cruel Egyptians. They talked about how Moses and Joshua had led them into the promised land where they now lived.

The people danced and sang all day long. David danced the hardest, though. All the joy and happiness he felt at being God's chosen king, and having God's ark close by, just overflowed into his arms and legs. He bounced around, twisted and turned. He did somersaults and sang as loud as he could.

"Let the heavens rejoice, let the earth be glad. Let the sea roar, and all that's in it! Let the fields be happy! Then the trees of the forest will sing. They will sing for joy before the Lord!"

David was very happy, but his wife Michal was not. Michal, who was Saul's daughter, watched from the window. "Why is David being so silly?" she thought to herself.

That night when she saw him, she told David she was ashamed of him. Despite their earlier love for each other, David and Michal were never close again. And Michal never had any children.

151

David Becomes a Murderer

2 Samuel 11:1-26

King David was a very great king because he loved God so much. One day, though, David stopped putting God first in his life.

Instead, he chose to go to bed with a married woman. This was against God's rules. The woman's name was Bathsheba. She was the wife of Uriah the Hittite. He was one of David's most trusted soldiers.

When David found out that Bathsheba was carrying his baby, he felt desperate. All he wanted to do was cover up his wrong.

David had his general send Uriah to where the fighting was the worst. Then the general was supposed to pull the rest of his troops back so Uriah could be killed by the enemy.

When news of Uriah's death reached Bathsheba, she cried and cried for many days. She had loved her husband. She felt very hurt by all that had happened.

The Broken King

2 Samuel 11:27-12:24

Some time after Uriah's death, David sent a message to Bathsheba. He wanted her to become his wife. Bathsheba went to the palace. She married David. A few months later their baby boy was born.

David and Bathsheba may have been glad they had a son, but God was not happy. He knew David had done a wicked thing. David could not hide from God. David had not only taken another man's wife, he had killed her husband!

So the Lord sent His prophet Nathan to see David. Nathan told David, "The Lord says, because you have done this thing, your sons will fight each other and this child will die."

David hung his head. The Lord's words pierced his heart like a sword. He knew God was right. The wrong he had done could never be kept secret from God. David said, "I'm so sorry, Lord. I should never have done this wrong thing."

The baby did die. But a year later David and Bathsheba had a second son. They named this boy Solomon. He was a very special boy. Solomon had been chosen by God to become the wisest man who ever lived.

153

The Young King

1 Kings 3:2-5; 2 Chronicles 1:7-8

When David died, young Solomon became king. To be a king with gold and jewels may sound very fine. To be a king who knows what is best for the people, that is very, very hard. When Solomon became king, he did not feel very sure of himself.

Then one night, Solomon had a dream. God appeared to Solomon. He said, "Ask whatever you wish from Me and I will give it to you."

Some people might have asked for more toys, good health, more money or power. Solomon did not ask for any of these things. Instead he wanted something far, far better.

Solomon's Dream

1 Kings 3:6-15; 2 Chronicles 1:9-13

When God asked Solomon to make a wish, Solomon answered, "Lord, You helped my father David while he was king. He trusted in You. Now You have made me king in his place. I'm so very young, Lord. I don't know how to be a good king like my father David was. I only ask for this one thing. Give me a heart full of wisdom. Help me to see what is right and wrong. I want to rule over Your people as You want. Help me to judge Your people with wisdom. Help me to know the difference between good and bad."

This answer pleased God very much. He said to Solomon, "Because

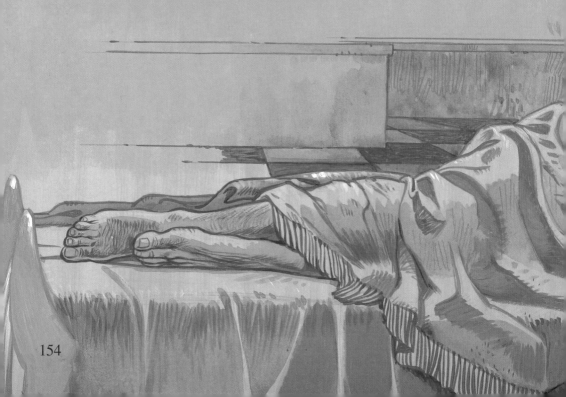

you have asked for this and not to live a long life or become rich, I will make your wish come true. Now I have given you a wise heart. There will never be a king as wise or as great as you."

But that was not all. God added, "I have also given you what you have not asked for. You have riches and honour. If you walk in My ways, I will see that you live a long life."

155

The Baby with Two Mothers

1 Kings 3:16-28

One day two mothers came to King Solomon. Each carried a baby. The first woman's baby was dead. The second woman's was alive. Each woman claimed the living baby as her own.

Solomon said, "Guard, cut the living child in two. Then give half to one woman and half to the other."

The first woman screamed, "No! Please, don't! You'll kill him. Oh, my lord, give her the baby. Then at least he'll stay alive."

But the second woman said, "You're right, King Solomon. Go on, cut him in half! Then neither of us will have him!"

The king sighed and told his guard, "Give the living baby to the first woman. She spoke as only the true mother could have."

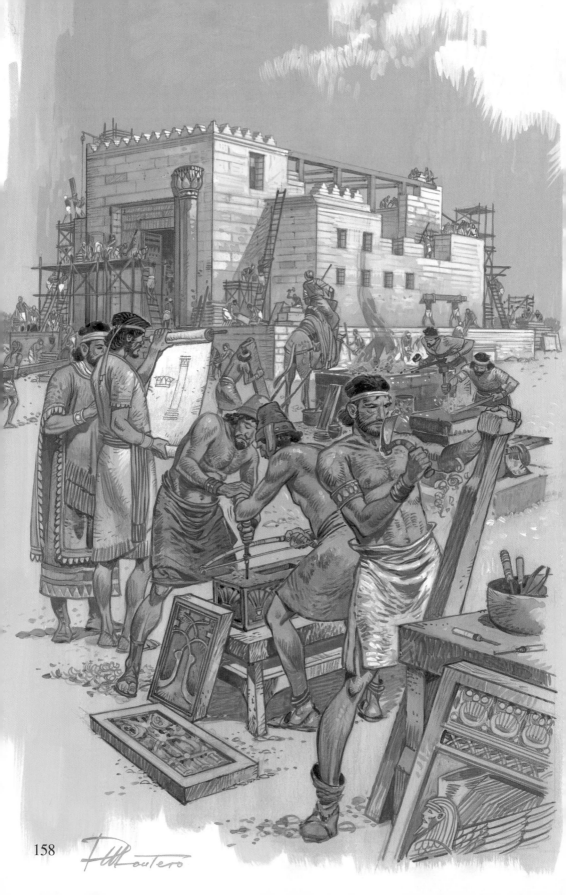

158

A Temple for the Lord

1 Kings 4:20-28; 6:1-38; 7:1-12; 8:1-9:28; 10:14-29;
2 Chronicles 1:14-8:18; 9:13-28; Psalm 72

Perhaps the most important thing
Solomon did was to build the temple of
God in Jerusalem. The huge building
took seven years to build. It would last
four hundred years.

Cedar wood and gold covered the
temple, inside and out. The best
bronze smiths, artists and sculptors
made beautiful figures. They covered
the ceiling and walls with bright
designs.

When the temple was finished,
Solomon called together all of God's
chosen people. The priests brought the
ark containing the Ten
Commandments. They placed it in a
special room inside the temple. A
cloud which covered the Lord came
down upon the temple then. The
people knew the Lord was very close
to them.

Solomon prayed, "God, thank You
that I was able to build this temple for
You. Thank You that my father David
planned it. But even this temple is not
good enough. No place is big or high
enough for You. You made the earth
and the sky. Please, Lord, let this
temple be a place where we can always
find You."

Afterwards God appeared to
Solomon. He said, "If you do what I
tell you, I will live in this temple. I will
listen to the prayers of the people who
come into this place."

Solomon also built a magnificent
palace for himself. This palace took
thirteen years to finish. His throne
room was like no other, made of gold
and jewels.

Then he built a beautiful palace for
one of his many wives. This was the
daughter of the Egyptian pharaoh.
Solomon needed many workers for
these building projects. All the men
who belonged to former enemy tribes
became Solomon's workers, as did his
own people.

Solomon was very rich. Every day
he ate out of golden bowls and plates.
He used golden knives and forks. His
cups were made of gold. Even his
clothes had golden threads sewn into
the fabric.

The most important part of
Solomon's reign was how he judged
the people with fairness. He wrote,
"Let the mountains bring peace to the
people. . . . May the king . . . save
the children of the needy and crush
the one who hurts them." More than
anything else, Solomon wanted to take
good care of God's people. He was
able to do this, as long as he followed
God's laws.

The Visit of the Queen of Sheba

1 Kings 4:29-34; 10:1-13; 2 Chronicles 9:1-12

Word of Solomon's wealth and wisdom spread far and wide. The queen of Sheba came from a land which is now called Yemen. This queen had heard of Solomon's greatness. She did not believe the stories. She came all that way just to test him and see for herself if the stories were true.

The queen travelled with many camels. They carried spices and gold and diamonds and rubies. When she arrived at Solomon's palace, she asked him every question she could think of.

The wisdom which God gave Solomon had stretched his heart and mind. He could see a problem from all the different sides and tell which was the right side.

The queen said, "What I heard about you was only half true. You're even wiser and richer than the stories claim!"

Then she gave Solomon many gifts of spices and precious stones. Never again would so many spices come into Israel at one time. There were cinnamon, salt, nutmeg, cloves, pepper and many, many other spices. All of these were rare and precious. She also gave Solomon great amounts of gold. King Solomon gave the queen of Sheba many special gifts as well.

Finally the queen said farewell to her friend. She returned to her own land, very far away. With her went the tales, even more fantastic than before, of Solomon's wisdom.

The Contest

1 Kings 16:29-33; 17:1; 18:19-36

There once was a prophet named Elijah. A prophet is someone chosen by God to speak His words. A prophet's message is meant to bring people closer to God . . . but they must be willing to listen.

Elijah lived in a time much later than King Solomon. While Elijah was alive the people of God were worshipping other gods. Their king and queen were called Ahab and Jezebel. These two were very bad. They had led the people away from God.

Elijah finally challenged the priests of Jezebel to a contest. He told King Ahab, "You were wrong to follow this false god Baal. Send me eight hundred and fifty of the prophets who eat at your wife's table. Then we will see whose god is for real!"

The time had come for God to work a miracle so great, His people could no longer doubt who the true God was. For the last three years, the people had heard their king and queen say, "Baal will bring you rain. Just wait and see."

No matter how much the people sacrificed and prayed, though, no rain had fallen. That was because Baal was a nothing god. Only the Lord God could bring rain to the thirsty land. He wanted to prove to the people through Elijah that He was the only God they should worship.

Elijah told the priests of Baal to kill a bull. They should lay it on the wood, but put no fire under it. He would do the same with his bull and pile of wood. "Call on your god to light a fire under the bull, and I will call on my God! The God who answers with fire is the real God."

All the people agreed that this was a very fair test. The priests of Baal tried and tried. They prayed from morning until noon, "Oh Baal, answer us." But there was no answer. They danced and shouted louder and louder. They jumped around the altar. But still there was no answer. No fire burned the wood beneath their bull.

Then it was Elijah's turn. He had four large jars of water poured over the altar. He did this three times until the trench was full. Then he poured water over his pile of wood, under the dead bull.

162

163

Fire and Rain

1 Kings 18:37-46

Elijah lifted his hands up toward
heaven. He prayed calmly and slowly,
so everyone could hear. "Oh Lord, the
God of Abraham, Isaac and Israel,
show us that You are God. I am Your
servant. Answer me, Lord. Show this
people that You are Lord. Please
answer now with Your fire, I pray!"

Suddenly the fire of the Lord fell
from heaven! All the wood and stones
and dust and parts of the bull were

eaten up by the fire. The heat was terrible. It did not matter that everything was wet, it caught fire anyway.

"Look! Fire is falling from the sky!" the crowds screamed. The people yelled, "The Lord, He is God!"

King Ahab's knees knocked together in fear. Elijah told him, "Go, eat and drink, for I hear the roar of thunder."

Ahab did as he was told. He hurried home before anything more terrible happened. Now that the people of Israel had said they believed the Lord was God, Elijah hoped God would bring rain.

He told his servant to watch for clouds. At first there was nothing. Time after time Elijah told his servant to go and look. Finally the servant said, "Look! There's a cloud the size of a man's hand. It's coming up from the sea!"

Within moments, the sky grew black with clouds and wind. Water poured down. The people raised their hands and cheered. Finally, after three years, they had rain!

But God worked yet one more miracle. As the rain gushed down from the clouds, Elijah started running across the countryside. He ran as fast as he could. The hand of the Lord was on Elijah! God's Spirit came upon Elijah in power. He turned him into a super-runner! He ran faster than the horses pulling King Ahab's chariot. He ran faster than the wind. Elijah ran so fast, he arrived in Jezreel before the king did!

The Chariot of Fire

2 Kings 2:1-12

Elijah had become a very old man. All his life he tried to lead the people back to God. Elijah had a young friend named Elisha.

The time had come for Elijah to die and go to heaven. Elijah had promised Elisha a double portion of his power as prophet. Elisha had to make sure he was watching, when God took Elijah to heaven.

While they were still walking and talking together, a fiery chariot with blinding horses came between them! It blazed like the sun, as bright as fire. Flaming horses pulled the chariot. A huge blast of wind swept Elijah off the ground. He was taken up to heaven!

It looked like a great whirlwind. When Elisha saw it, he cried out, "My father, my father!" But Elijah had gone to be with God.

A Strange Way to Cross a River

2 Kings 2:13-15

Elisha stood watching as the prophet Elijah was taken up to heaven. It was an amazing sight! Fiery horses ran across the sky. They pulled a chariot so bright, it could have been on fire. Elijah rode in the fiery chariot. Wind howled in Elisha's ears. He shaded his eyes with his hands, the light was so bright. Sand blew in a whirlwind around him.

Then suddenly it was very quiet. Elisha lowered his hands and looked up. Elijah was gone. The sky was empty, the wind still. Elisha looked around him. He was alone.

He bent down and picked up Elijah's cloak. Then he turned to face the Jordan River. He took the cloak and struck the waters.

"Where is the Lord, the God of Elijah?" he called out. As Elisha struck the water with Elijah's cloak, water reared up into a wall of waves. Elisha crossed over a strip of dry land. When he reached the other side, the waves came down with a crash.

Elisha's wish had come true. God had given him the same spirit of a prophet as Elijah had had. Elisha the prophet was ready to go wherever God called him.

169

The Bottomless Jar of Oil

2 Kings 4:1-7

Elisha travelled up and down the land.
Everywhere he preached to the people.
He tried to make them stop
worshipping false gods. He gave advice
to kings and poor people. Elisha told
everyone he met about God's love.
Because the Holy Spirit was with
Elisha, he worked miracles in God's
name.

One such miracle helped save a
mother and her two boys from being
sold as slaves. This woman was the
widow of a prophet for God. When
the evil Queen Jezebel was still in
power, many men of God had been
killed. This woman was the wife of
one such dead prophet. She had two
little children to take care of, but no
money.

In those days it was very hard for a
widow to make any money. This
woman had no one to help her.
"Please sir!" she cried out to Elisha.
"My husband is dead. You know he
obeyed and trusted in God. But I owe
so much money. And I have nothing
to pay with. The man I owe money to
says he will come and take my
children away if I don't pay him soon.
My children and I will become slaves!
Please help me!"

Elisha said, "How can I help?"
Then he thought for a moment. "Tell
me, what do you have in your house?

Is there anything you can sell to make some money?"

The woman shook her head sadly. Her hair fell in her face. She hugged her two boys. "I have nothing but a jar of oil."

Elisha said, "Go, and ask your neighbours for empty jars. Don't ask for a few. Bring every jar you can find. Then bring them back to your house. Take your sons with you and shut the door. Pour out the oil of your one jar into all the jars you have collected. Then set them to one side."

She did as Elisha told her. She went around to all her neighbours. She collected as many jars as she could. Then she closed the door and started pouring oil.

She poured and poured and poured and poured. First one jar was full, then another and another and another. The little jar of oil from which she poured seemed bottomless. How could it contain so much oil? Finally, she said to her son, "Bring me another jar."

But he answered, "That was the last one."

The woman looked at the many, many jars of oil filling her house. She shook her head in wonder. She went to tell Elisha what had happened. He said, "Go, sell the oil and pay your debt. Then you and your sons can live off the rest of the money."

Runaway from God

Jonah 1:1-3

There once was a man called Jonah. He was one of God's people, the Israelites. One day God said to Jonah, "I want you to go to the city of Nineveh. Tell them they are living such wicked lives, I will have to punish them."

Jonah did not like Nineveh. The people of Nineveh were enemies of God's people.

But God was willing to forgive the Ninevites if they would just change their ways. The Ninevites were the cruellest people in the world at that time. If God could forgive them, He could forgive anyone.

Jonah did not like this. "Why should God care about them?" he wondered. So Jonah did a foolish thing. He ignored God. He ran away from Nineveh, rather than toward it. That way, the Ninevites would not be warned about how angry God was with them. Jonah wanted the Ninevites to be destroyed.

But Jonah had made a mistake. There is no place where people can hide from God. He is everywhere and knows everything.

Jonah went down to the harbour, a place called Joppa. That is where the city of Tel-Aviv now stands.

In Joppa, Jonah wandered up and down the docks. He was looking for a ship which would take him clear to the other side of the world. Jonah found one headed for Tarshish. That was far enough.

He went as far from Nineveh as

possible. Once the ship set sail, Jonah breathed a sigh of relief. "Now those evil Ninevites will get what they deserve," he thought to himself.

Storm at Sea

Jonah 1:4-16

Once on board, Jonah fell asleep. He thought he could relax because he had run away from God. He was wrong.

The Lord threw a great wind at the sea. A terrible storm shook the waves. The ship was tossed up and down and rocked from one side to the other. The sailors said, "There must be some reason why this is happening. Someone on the ship must have made his god angry!"

So each sailor prayed to his own god, begging to be saved. The wind howled louder. The waves reared higher and higher.

The captain went below deck and shook Jonah. "How can you be sleeping through a storm like this?" he asked. "You should be praying to your God. Maybe He will be able to save us."

When the men on board heard that Jonah was a Jew, they became very frightened. They had heard about this Lord God of Israel. They gasped, "You tried to run away from Him?" Even they knew that was impossible. God sees everything.

"It is your God who is punishing us. Now tell us, how do we stop this storm?"

Jonah said, "If you throw me overboard, the storm will go away."

At first the sailors would not throw Jonah into the sea. But they had no choice. They prayed to Jonah's God, "Oh, Lord. Please don't kill us with this storm. We haven't done anything wrong. Only this man has." They had no choice. They picked up Jonah and threw him into the raging sea. Suddenly, the wind stopped howling. The waves died down.

The Big Fish

Jonah 1:17-2:10

When the sailors threw him overboard, Jonah felt something cold and slimy bump up against him. He would have screamed with fright if he had not been underwater. A giant fish was swimming around him!

Suddenly, the fish opened its mouth wide and "Swoosh!" Jonah was swept into its mouth. The fish had swallowed Jonah!

Because the fish was so large, Jonah could stand up inside and breathe again. It was very dark and smelled sour.

It was not by chance that the fish had swallowed Jonah. God had chosen this fish to teach Jonah a lesson. No matter where he went, he could never run away from God. God wanted Jonah to do what He had been told and go to Nineveh with the Lord's message.

After a while, Jonah asked God to forgive him for trying to run away. He thanked the Lord for not forgetting him.

After three days and three nights, the Lord made the fish spit Jonah out of its stomach. There was a great wet rush. Jonah held his breath again as he swirled around inside the fish's mouth. The next thing he knew, he was lying on a dry beach.

174

Jonah Changes His Mind

Jonah 3:1-10

For a second time the Lord told Jonah, "Now go to Nineveh and give them My message."

This time Jonah did as he was told. Nineveh was huge. Homes spread out for miles around. It took Jonah three days to walk around the city. All that time he called out, "In forty days Nineveh will be destroyed!"

The people of Nineveh heard Jonah and were shocked. This was terrible news! They listened to God's warnings. They believed in God. They took off their rich clothes and wore plain clothing, made of sackcloth. They stopped eating and spent their days praying. Everyone from the poorest beggar to the richest farmer asked God to forgive them for living such evil lives.

Even the king of Nineveh laid aside his robe and put on the sackcloth clothes. He ordered everybody to do the same. "No one may eat, not even the animals!"

When God saw how all the people were sorry and wanted to change, He forgave them.

God Is Good

Jonah 4:1-11

When God decided to let the people of Nineveh live, Jonah was not very happy. "Lord, how could You save Nineveh, that awful city and all those evil people! It just isn't fair!"

The Lord said, "Jonah, what is the matter? Why are you so upset?"

Jonah went off to a place east of the city to sulk. That day, Jonah sat in the hot sun, waiting and watching. God caused a plant to grow so that it shaded Jonah from the sunlight. Thanks to the plant, he could look out over the city without becoming too hot. Jonah thought this plant was the only good thing in his life.

But God had a worm attack the plant and by sunrise the next day, it had withered. God called the hot east wind to blow and the sun to beat down on Jonah's head. That day he became faint and begged with all his might, "Please Lord, I am furious at this plant. Even it has failed me. Please put me out of my pain."

God asked Jonah, "Why should you be angry at the plant?"

Jonah said, "I want that plant back."

Then the Lord said, "You are angry because this plant died. You wanted it to live, even though you did not plant it. It came up one night and died the next. Now why shouldn't I care for the over one hundred thousand people in Nineveh? They did not know until you told them that what they were doing was so wrong.

"This was the reason I sent you to them. They needed to learn the difference between good and bad. Now, through you, they have met Me."

Jonah finally realized, God had taught him a very big lesson.

177

Jeremiah Stays Behind

2 Kings 25:8-24; 2 Chronicles 36:18-21; Jeremiah 39:8-14; 40:1-6; 52:12-30

For many, many years now, God had sent prophets to warn His people. If they did not stop praying to false gods, they would become weak. Jerusalem would be destroyed. God's people would become slaves. But the people had not listened.

Now the time had come for the Babylonian king, Nebuchadnezzar, to capture and destroy Jerusalem. Nebuchadnezzar had ordered his soldiers to set fire to the temple of the Lord. He burned the king's palace. He burned all the houses of Jerusalem. Any building worth anything at all, the Babylonians set on fire. The entire city went up in flames!

Then his army broke down the walls of Jerusalem and captured all the people. They made them into slaves and sent them to Babylon.

While Jerusalem burned, King Nebuchadnezzar sent his men into the palaces and temple to strip them of treasure. With buildings burning all around them, his soldiers grabbed

every piece of gold and silver they saw. There was nothing left of the temple! Nebuchadnezzar carried it all away to Babylon, even the huge bronze pillars.

God's prophet at this time was a man named Jeremiah. Except for the poor, he was the only man Nebuchadnezzar spared. Nebuchadnezzar gave orders that he should not be harmed. One of the king's captains told Jeremiah, "Everything has happened just as you said it would. The Lord has brought disaster on this place because the people didn't listen. But now you are free. Come with us to Babylon where you'll be safe, or stay here. Go wherever you want."

When Jeremiah did not choose to go with the king's bodyguard to Babylon, the captain said, "All right, stay here with the people." Then he gave Jeremiah some food and money and let him go. Jeremiah chose to stay with God's people. These were the poorest of the poor, all that was left of the ruined city Jerusalem.

A Special School

Daniel 1:1-6

King Nebuchadnezzar captured several
groups of Jews. He made them into
slaves and forced them to live in
Babylon. The last group were made
prisoners when Jerusalem was set on
fire and destroyed. Among the first
group, taken eighteen years earlier,
were young men from rich families in
Judah. One was a boy named Daniel.

Daniel and three of his friends came
from leading Jewish families. King
Nebuchadnezzar had ordered that, of
the prisoners, the best-looking,
strongest and cleverest boys should be
put in a special school. There they
would be taught three years by
Babylonian teachers. After that, the
best of the best would get to work for
the king himself.

Now Daniel and his friends did not
have to be slaves anymore. But they
did have to try and please the
Babylonians. And because they were
Jewish, because they were different,
sometimes this was hard to do.

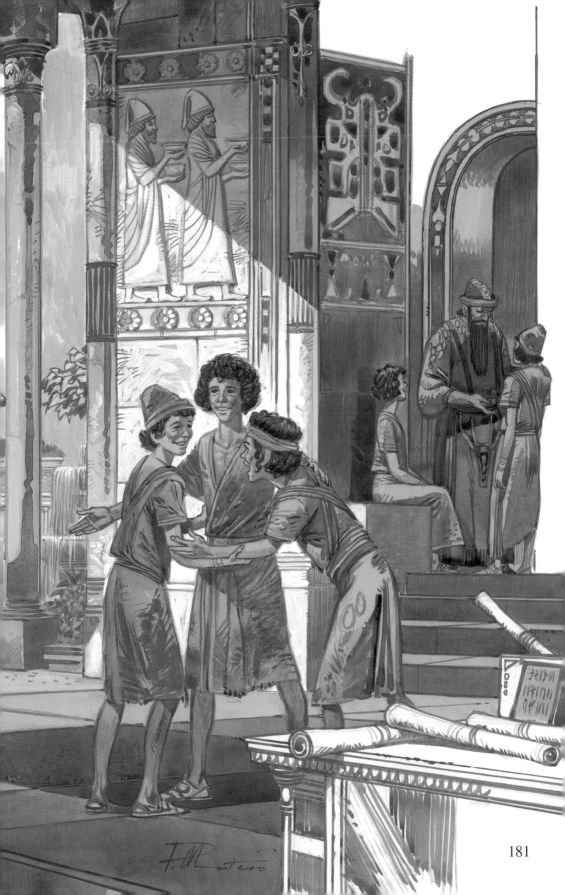

Being Different

Daniel 1:7-8

Daniel and his friends knew they were different. They didn't mind. They were proud to be members of God's chosen people.

Daniel's friends were called Hananiah, Mishael and Azariah. Together they were the cleverest of all the boys brought to Babylon. The Babylonians made these boys study the history and books and language of Babylon. And they gave them Babylonian names.

The king's chief, a man named Ashpenaz, renamed the boys. Daniel became Belteshazzar. Hananiah became Shadrach. Mishael was called Meshach. Azariah was renamed Abed-nego.

King Nebuchadnezzar ordered the boys to eat only the best of foods. They were supposed to eat plenty of fresh vegetables and meat, as well as drink wine every day.

There was only one problem, though. The meat and wine which the Babylonians gave to Daniel and his friends were not the sort which God's people were allowed to have. The laws which God had given Moses said Jews could eat only certain types of meat. This meat had to come from animals which had been killed in certain ways.

Daniel and his friends had learned these rules as little boys, when they still lived with their families back in Jerusalem. Daniel made up his mind that he would not break the rules God had given His people.

A Test of Faith

Daniel 1:9-13

Daniel went to Ashpenaz. He pointed at the food on the table. "Please sir, I've come to ask your help. I can't follow the king's orders."

Ashpenaz looked at the boy standing before him. God had warmed the heart of Ashpenaz toward Daniel. As he listened, he already knew he would help this boy, no matter what the cost.

"But Daniel, you can't do that. If the king finds out I haven't fed you as he ordered, he'll have me killed. What will I do when he sees your faces looking paler and thinner than those of the other boys?"

Daniel was quiet for a moment. Then he smiled, "I know!"

He ran over to the guard Ashpenaz had chosen for him. "Could you give me and my friends ten days? Feed us only vegetables and give us only water to drink. When ten days are up, see if we look better or worse than the other boys who get the king's special food. After that you can decide what we should eat." The guard looked over at Ashpenaz. He nodded. The contest began.

Passing the Test

Daniel 1:14-20

The guard kept his word. For ten days
he let Daniel, Hananiah, Mishael and
Azariah eat only vegetables and drink
only water. At the end of that time the
four boys did exercises in front of
Ashpenaz.

Ashpenaz could not believe his
eyes! Daniel and his friends had
gained more weight than the other
boys! Not only that, their eyes
sparkled. Their smiles shone. The
other boys were out of breath, while
Daniel and his friends still had plenty
of energy left!

Ashpenaz told the guard that for the
rest of the three years the boys could
eat only vegetables and drink only
water. God continued to bless them
and they grew big and strong.

God also helped the four boys
become very clever and wise. They
learned all they could about the books,
history and language of Babylon.
Daniel could even tell people what
their dreams meant.

When three years were over,
Ashpenaz brought the boys to King
Nebuchadnezzar. The king tested them
on all they had learned. He asked
them many hard questions. Of all the
boys there, the best and wisest answers
were always given by Daniel,
Hananiah, Mishael and Azariah. So
the king himself chose them to be his
advisers.

The Wizards

Daniel 2:1-13

Soon after Daniel became the king's adviser, King Nebuchadnezzar kept having a terrible dream. He called all his wizards. "This dream upsets me. I want to know what it means."

The wizards said, "Yes, Your Majesty. Tell us your dream and we'll find out what it means."

But the king answered, "No. You must first tell me what I dreamt, then what it meant. If you can't do this, you and your homes will be torn in pieces. If you can do this thing, I'll give you rich gifts and great honour."

The wizards thought maybe they had not heard right. So they said again, "Let the king tell us his dream. Then we'll be glad to tell him what it means."

The king grew angry. "Oh no you don't! You're just trying to trick me. Now listen! You tell me my dream and then you can tell me what it means!"

"But no king has ever asked this of his magicians!"

The king became even angrier. He stood up and pointed at all the wizards whining and mumbling in front of him. "Enough! If you cannot follow this order, then I'll have you killed!" So the order went out to kill all the king's wise men.

But the order included more than just the wizards. It meant all the king's advisers. That meant Daniel and his friends would be killed too!

What Does the King's Dream Mean?

Daniel 2:14-43

Daniel and his friends prayed together. Late that night, Daniel had a vision. He thanked the Lord, then ran to see the king.

"Can you really tell me what I dreamt. Can you say what it means?" the king asked.

Daniel said, "No. But there is a God in heaven who can. You saw a horrible statue. Its head was made of gold, its chest and arms were made of silver, its waist and hips of bronze, its legs of iron and its feet of both iron and clay.

"A great stone broke loose from a cliff and destroyed the statue, piece by piece. The stone grew to become a mountain which covered the whole earth.

"That was the dream. The meaning is this. Each part of the statue is a different kingdom. You, as king of Babylon, are the head. After you will come another kingdom, and then another. Finally a fourth kingdom, as strong as iron, will rule. But it will be a divided kingdom."

A Never-Ending Kingdom

Daniel 2:44-49

God had shown the king how Babylon would fall to Persia. Later, Greece would rule the area, followed by Rome. Rome was the divided empire. Then God would work the greatest miracle of all, using His own Son, Jesus. His would be a different kingdom, based on peace, not war. Daniel went on to talk about this time, so very far in the future.

"While the divided kingdom rules, God will set up another kingdom which can never be destroyed. It will last forever. That is the great stone, cut from the mountain by the same great God who has shown these things to the king."

The king said to Daniel, "Your God is truly the greatest and wisest!" Then the king made Daniel the most powerful man in Babylon, next to the king himself.

189

Three Brave Men

Daniel 3:1-18

Many years passed. King Nebuchadnezzar soon forgot what he had said about Daniel's God being the only one. Instead he built a giant statue of gold. He called this his god.

He sent out an order, "Whenever the royal music is played, everyone must fall to the ground and pray to this statue. Anyone who doesn't, will be thrown into a blazing furnace to die."

Before long the king's men noticed that the three best friends of Daniel were not praying to the golden statue. If they had, they would have broken God's law. This law said, "I am the Lord your God. I will be your only God. Do not make statues and worship them."

When Nebuchadnezzar heard this, he sent for Daniel's friends. He called them by their Babylonian names. "Shadrach, Meshach and Abed-nego, is it true you will not worship my statue?"

The three men stood firm. "We can never worship your god. Even if we are thrown into the blazing furnace, our God is able to save us from it."

The Blazing Furnace

Daniel 3:19-30

Nebuchadnezzar burned with anger. He ordered his soldiers to tie up the three men. "Take them away! And see that the fire is seven times hotter than usual!"

The soldiers threw Daniel's friends into the furnace. When they did, though, it was so very hot, the soldiers were the ones who died! Then the king saw something which was even more amazing.

The three men were no longer tied up! They could walk between the flames. They did not suffer at all. But even more astounding, a fourth man was with them. He shone brighter than the fire itself. Could this have been Jesus Himself, sent by His Father to comfort the three men?

The king ordered the men to come out. When they walked out of the fire, the fourth man had disappeared. Daniel's friends were safe!

The king shook his head. "Incredible! Surely your God is the greatest. He protects those who trust Him. From now on, no one is allowed to say anything bad about your God."

The King's Feast

Daniel 5:1-12

King Nebuchadnezzar lived to be an old man and then he died. The next king of Babylon was a man named Belshazzar. Daniel continued to work as the king's adviser. One day, when Daniel was an old man, a strange thing happened.

The king was throwing a big party. He was drunk and having a good time. Then he thought he would do something different, just for fun. He wanted to see all the gold and silver cups and plates that had been taken out of God's temple in Jerusalem.

"Tonight we will drink like the gods!" he told his guests. Together they praised the false gods of gold and silver. Then they drank out of the holy cups.

Suddenly, all at once, a strange hand came out of nowhere! It began writing on the wall of the king's palace. The king turned pale. His hand shook. He felt his knees knock.

"Quickly!" he called. "Bring the wizards, magicians and wise men here. I have to know what this hand has written. I'll give anyone who can read it a great reward!" All the wizards tried their best, but nobody could read the writing on the wall.

"Your Majesty," the queen mother said. "There is a man who might help you. He is the head of the wise men. He helped Nebuchadnezzar interpret his dreams. This Daniel might be able to help you now."

Writing on the Wall

Daniel 5:13-31

Daniel was brought before the king, who said, "I've heard you know what dreams mean. Tell me what this horrible hand has written on the wall. Then you will be greatly rewarded. You may wear the royal colour purple and I'll give you a gold necklace."

"You can keep your gifts," Daniel said. "I don't want your rewards. I'll read the meaning of these words because of what the Most High God shows me. Do you remember the lesson King Nebuchadnezzar had to learn? He knew that God is the One who decides who should be king.

"But you haven't learned this. You haven't shown respect for the Lord. That was what King Nebuchadnezzar once ordered. You've grown so proud that you took the cups and plates from God's temple. You gave them to your women to drink wine out of. That's why this hand has written a message for you today.

"The words mean this: God will soon end your kingdom. You have been judged and have failed the test. Your kingdom will be divided between the Medes and Persians."

When Daniel had finished, the king rewarded him. Then that same night, all that Daniel had said came true. Belshazzar was killed and the Persians conquered the Babylonian empire.

193

The Lions' Den

Daniel 6:1-28

After Belshazzar was killed, Darius the Mede became king. Darius put three men in charge of his kingdom. One of these three men was Daniel.

Daniel had become a very old man. He had served God with all his heart and mind and strength. He was a man of prayer. Daniel had seen God do mighty things. And the Lord had blessed Daniel with wisdom.

Soon Darius noticed that Daniel was better than the other two advisers. The king wanted to put Daniel in charge of the entire kingdom.

This did not make the other advisers very happy. They plotted against Daniel. They tried to find something Daniel had done wrong. They wanted to prove he was a liar or a cheat. This was hard to do since Daniel was a good man. Finally, the king's men came up with a way they could trap Daniel.

Together they went to the king. "Your Majesty, we think you should sign this order. It says you are a god. For the next thirty days, any man who prays to other gods must be thrown into the lions' den and die." The king liked the idea. So he signed the order.

Even though Daniel knew about the king's order, he continued praying to the Lord. All his life he had prayed at least three times a day. Kneeling by a window which faced Jerusalem, Daniel thanked God for all His blessings. He prayed for his people. He hoped the time would soon come when the Jews could go back to Jerusalem.

Daniel's enemies saw him praying from the street below. Then they went to the king. "Remember the order you gave about not worshipping any god but you? Well, Daniel has broken that law! He still prays to his God every day."

When the king heard this, he knew he had been tricked. All day long he tried to come up with a way of saving Daniel. There was nothing he could do. The order was signed and sealed.

The guards brought Daniel to him. The king said, "There's nothing I can do. I hope your God will save you." Then Daniel was thrown into the great pit with the wild lions! The hole was covered with a huge stone. What would happen to him? Was this the end?

The next day, as soon as the sun rose, the king hurried to the lions' den. He stood over the stone which filled the hole. His voice shook. "Daniel, servant of the living God! Has your God been able to rescue you from the lions?" He held his breath.

There was a voice answering! "Your Majesty, yes He has!" Daniel was safe! "My God sent His angel and shut the lions' mouths. God protected me and I'm not hurt. I haven't done anything

wrong, Your Majesty!"

The king called at once for the guards to open the den. When they lifted Daniel out, there was not even a scratch on him. The king sent for the men who had tricked and trapped Daniel. He told his guards to throw these men into the lions' den. The evil advisers did not even reach the bottom of the pit before the lions finished them off.

The king ordered, "Everywhere in my kingdom people are to respect the God of Daniel. He is the living God. His kingdom will last forever. He does signs and wonders. He saved Daniel from the power of the lions!"

195

The Proud King

Esther 1:1-8; 2:5-7

Not all the Jews captured by the Babylonians ended up in the royal city. Many settled elsewhere in the Persian empire. This is where a beautiful Jewish girl named Esther lived. She had no parents and lived with her cousin, a man called Mordecai.

One of the kings of Persia was a man named Ahasuerus. His kingdom stretched from Egypt to Africa and included India.

King Ahasuerus was a very proud king. He liked nothing better than to show people how great and powerful he was. He spent half a year showing all the important people in his kingdom just how rich and mighty he was. They had seen his treasures and his palace, his horses and his armies. At the end of that time he gave a feast which lasted seven days.

All the people came to the king's garden party. They sat on couches made of gold and silver and precious gems. They looked at wall hangings woven with threads of gold. They drank wine out of golden cups. They talked and danced around the fountains.

Queen Vashti's Refusal

Esther 1:19-22

King Ahasuerus bragged, "I'm the richest king ever. My armies are the greatest. And, I have the world's most beautiful queen!"

"Ah," sighed the crowd. They had heard of Queen Vashti. "Show her to us! We want to see the queen!" the people chanted.

The king's servants ran to where Queen Vashti was having her own party. They told her, "The king has ordered you to come before his guests."

The queen sighed and put her hands on her hips. "Why?"

"He wants to show them how beautiful you are."

But to their amazement, the queen shook her head. "No. Tell him I'll come later. Can't you see I'm busy right now?"

The servants were shocked. They hurried back to the king with the news. His guests were shocked. Everyone watched King Ahasuerus to see what he would do. The king was furious! He called for his advisers. He said, "How should I punish the queen for not doing what I told her?"

His advisers said, "You must act quickly. Otherwise all the wives of all the princes in the kingdom will start saying no to their husbands. The men won't like that! Send out a royal order that Vashti is no longer your queen. Then look for someone else to take

her place."

The king liked this idea. He sent out the order. It was written in many different languages. Everyone understood. The king was looking for a new queen.

Miss Persia

Esther 2:1-20

King Ahasuerus sent out his most trusted men. They searched for the prettiest girls in the kingdom. Among them was the Jewish girl Esther.

Esther and the other young women were brought to the palace. There they climbed the front steps to their new home. They were given the best of everything, the most beautiful clothes and perfumes. Servants massaged them and fed them. They even dressed and put their makeup on for them. For an entire year the girls were treated like princesses.

While living in the palace, Esther made sure no one found out she was a Jew. This was something her cousin had told her to keep secret. Since Mordecai had always been like a father to her, Esther did as he said.

When the king's men took Esther to the palace, Mordecai had followed. Every morning for the next year, he paced the yard outside the palace. This way he could check on Esther.

When the year was up, it was time for the king to judge his very own beauty contest. Whichever girl won would become his new queen. Oh, the king enjoyed this very much indeed!

It was finally Esther's turn to meet the king. Everyone agreed, they had never seen a more beautiful young lady. Sure enough, the king said, "There is no one like Esther!" Lovely Esther was the new queen of Persia!

The Jews Must Die

Esther 2:21-3:15

Every day, Mordecai paced outside the palace. He waited to hear how Esther was. She was queen and could have anything she wanted. All the same, Mordecai still worried about her as if he were her father.

There was a very powerful man in the king's court called Haman. He was second only to the king himself. Haman ordered that whenever he passed by, people should kneel before him.

At the king's gate, though, there was one man who would not bow down. That was Mordecai! He knew Haman was an Amalekite, one of Israel's most hated enemies. There was no way he would bow down to an Amalekite.

Over and over again Haman walked by Mordecai. And over and over again Mordecai refused to bow down.

Haman grew angrier and angrier. Finally, Haman told the king, "There are people who do not obey orders. I will pay you to let me kill them all."

Haman did not want just Mordecai dead, he wanted all the Jews dead! And the king agreed, not even knowing who Haman was talking about! The king's scribes sent out letters to all of Persia. The orders were to kill every single Jew, young and old, women and children, and to do it within the year!

Esther Has a Plan

Esther 4:1-5:12

Mordecai was so upset about the order to kill the Jews, he tore off his clothes. He walked up and down the city streets, wailing.

He and Esther sent messages back and forth. Mordecai told her, "You must go to the king and beg for our lives."

Esther turned white with fear. "But the king sees only those people he sends for. If I visit him without being asked, he could have me killed. My only chance is if he holds out his golden sceptre and chooses to listen to me."

Mordecai was firm. He said, "You're not going to be saved just because you're the queen! If you stay quiet at a time like this, God will save His people through someone else. This is probably why you became queen."

Esther prayed. Then she said, "Tell Mordecai I've agreed. If I have to die, I will die."

Three days later, Esther entered the throne room. The king looked up and saw her. He smiled and held out the golden sceptre. "Ah, Esther. What is it? I would give you anything, even half my kingdom."

"If it pleases the king, I would like to invite you and Haman to eat dinner with me tonight." She waited and hoped.

"Why of course!" The king had agreed.

That evening, and the evening after, Esther ate with the king and Haman.

205

After the first meal, Haman went home and bragged to his friends. He showed them his money and said, "Why, I'm so great, even the king and queen eat with me."

Esther Saves Her People

Esther 7:1-6

It was the second time that Haman and the king had eaten with Esther. This was the moment she had been praying about. Once again, she had served only the best of the best. As the king looked at his lovely bride, he felt very pleased.

"Now tell me, my dear," he turned to Esther. "What is this all about? What is it that you want?"

Esther felt the push from inside her heart. She took a deep breath. "Please, I beg for my life, as well as the lives of my people. We are going to be destroyed. Killed. All of us!" Esther

bowed her head.

"How can this be?" the king cried. "What evil man would ever do this? Who is he?"

Esther sat up and pointed at Haman. "The wicked enemy is this man here! It is Haman!" Terrified, Haman choked on his wine.

Haman Is Hung

Esther 7:7-8:2

The king was furious. He stumbled out of the room and into Esther's garden. Haman threw himself at Esther's feet. He begged for mercy.

The king came back in the room. When he saw Haman clinging to Esther, he lost his temper. "You! How dare you attack the queen? Don't touch her like that!" The king's guards came running. They took one look and knew Haman was not going to live much longer.

The king said, "Hang this man!"

Then King Ahasuerus gave Haman's house and all he owned to Queen Esther. Mordecai came forward. Esther told the king how Mordecai was her cousin, but had loved her like a father.

The king took off his special ring and gave it to Mordecai. Then Esther gave all of Haman's property to Mordecai.

A Chance to Survive

Esther 8:3-17

After Mordecai received his reward, the queen went to the king for a second time. Again, she was risking her life. If the king did not hold out his golden sceptre, it meant she would die that very day.

As soon as Esther saw the king, she threw herself at his feet. She wept and sobbed. The king held out his golden sceptre. She was safe! "Oh, please! Is there any way my people can be saved from Haman's terrible order?"

Esther knew that once the king had ordered something, it could not be stopped. The king had an idea. He sent for Mordecai. "Mordecai, you have my ring now. Send out another order, one which can save the Jews."

Mordecai ordered, "All Jews are allowed to fight back when their enemies attack them on the battle day."

As the news spread, the Jews were overjoyed. Many people who were not Jews wanted to become Jews. They knew who the winner of the coming battle would be.

Fighting Back

Esther 9:1-10; 9:20-10:3

When the day of the battle came, it was the same day that Haman had set. But what happened was nowhere near what Haman had wanted. God blessed the Jews and made them into great fighters. The enemies of God's people were the ones who died that day, not the other way around! On the day of battle, all the princes and generals joined Mordecai's side. They helped God's people defend themselves against their enemies.

Then Mordecai sent out another order. This one said that Jews all over the kingdom should never, ever forget how God had helped them in strange and powerful ways. Every year they should remember and have a feast. Then everyone would give gifts of food to the poor.

After the feast Queen Esther went on to rule Persia by the side of the king for many, many years.

The New

An Angel Visits a Young Girl

Luke 1:26-38

The Jews knew that someday God would send a Messiah. The Messiah would bring God close to His people. This Messiah was Jesus. He came to earth as a baby and became the Saviour of the world.

Jesus' mother was a girl named Mary. One morning she woke up to a bright light. An angel named Gabriel entered Mary's room. "Hello, Mary, you are more special than any other woman!"

Mary felt scared. "Do not be afraid,

Testament

Mary. You have been chosen by God to be the mother of His Son, the Messiah."

Mary was going to marry a man called Joseph. When she heard the angel's words, she did not argue. Instead, Mary said, "Yes, I will do as you ask." She knew God would take care of her.

Gabriel told Mary that her friend Elizabeth was also going to have a baby. He added, "Nothing is impossible with God."

Mary believed him.

A Trip over the Mountains

Luke 1:5-25; 39-45

Mary's friend Elizabeth was a very, very old woman. She and her husband had wanted a baby for many years. Now finally, Elizabeth was going to have a baby. God had told her the baby would be very special.

After Gabriel visited Mary, she left her home in Nazareth, in Galilee. She travelled south to Judea to visit Elizabeth.

When Mary arrived, she called out, "Hello, Elizabeth!"

At the sound of Mary's voice, Elizabeth came running outside for the first time in months. She cried, "Mary, you are blessed by God. I just know you are the mother of my Lord! I know this because when you called out, my own baby jumped for joy inside me. You're so special, Mary! God's own Son lives inside you."

Beside the Well

Matthew 1:1-19

After visiting Elizabeth, Mary went home to Nazareth. She knew she would soon have to tell Joseph she was going to have a baby. She prayed that God would prepare him for the news. Mary loved Joseph and did not want to hurt him.

She sent word to him when she got home. She asked him to meet her at an old well just outside the village. When he arrived, Mary said, "Joseph, something amazing has happened. But it is true."

Joseph wondered why Mary looked so serious. Why was it so important that they meet where no one could

212

overhear them?

"Well," Mary continued, "God has blessed me very much. I don't really know why. He has chosen me to be the mother of the Messiah, His Son. The baby inside me is already three months old." Mary held her breath. She hoped Joseph would understand.

"Oh, Mary. . . ." Joseph turned away from her. "I love her so much," he thought. "But I can't make her my wife now." Joseph did not know if he should believe Mary.

He looked back at her again. Mary seemed so sure. Joseph walked away from the girl. He tried to think of ways he could call off the wedding without hurting Mary too much. They had built up so many hopes and dreams. Now they came crashing down around him.

Joseph's Dream

Matthew 1:20-24

One night soon afterwards, an angel of the Lord appeared to Joseph. "Son of David, do not be afraid to make Mary your wife. She speaks the truth. Her child will save His people from their sins. You should call Him Jesus."

When Joseph woke up, he chose to believe the message.

In the meantime Mary had been praying for Joseph. After Joseph had his dream he came to her. He said everything was all right. Her prayers were answered! A short time later, he and Mary were married.

Jesus Is Born

Matthew 1:25; Luke 2:1-7

It was very early in the morning. Joseph had packed the donkey. Mary climbed in between the bundles Joseph had strapped there. Together they set off for Bethlehem in Judea.

The Roman Emperor Caesar Augustus had told everyone to go back to the towns where their families came from. He wanted his soldiers to count the number of people in the tribes of Israel. Joseph's family came from Bethlehem, so that was where he had to go.

"I wish it were not today," Joseph said. "The baby is so near to being born."

Mary nodded. She was trying to stay on the donkey. It was not easy. The baby inside her was so large, she often lost her balance. "This will be a long day," she thought to herself.

The hours passed. When the sun rose, it became hot. Mary wanted to fall asleep. She knew she would fall off if she did. She walked for a little while. Soon she became so tired that Joseph put her back on the donkey.

Finally they arrived in Bethlehem. The streets were crowded. Children were running everywhere. There was so much noise! Suddenly, Mary felt a tightening in her stomach.

"Joseph, the baby. I think the baby is coming."

Joseph turned white. "We have to get you somewhere quiet, out of all these crowds," he said.

The couple went from house to house. They asked if anyone had a spare room. Nobody said yes.

At one point, Joseph cried, "Isn't there anywhere we can spend the night?"

"Well," one innkeeper said. "You could go behind the town. There, near the pastures, is a hillside. I keep my animals inside a deep cave there. Take her to the cave. Lay some fresh hay down. No one will bother you there.

At least it's quiet."

Joseph shouted his thanks over his shoulder. He ran back to Mary. She leaned on him as the two made their way out of town.

Once Mary was safe in the cave, Joseph relaxed. He had been praying so hard that all would go well. He felt bad that his wife would have her baby in a cave where animals lived. Mary and Joseph had no other choice, though.

When the baby was born, Joseph held the tiny baby boy in his arms. Mary said, "This is Jesus."

The Shepherds

Luke 2:8-17

During that first night when Jesus was born, a strange thing happened. In the nearby hills a group of shepherds slept outside. Suddenly, a loud noise woke them and they sat up.

"Look!" one cried. He pointed to the sky. The others looked up. There was a bright light, bigger than any star. It seemed to get bigger as it came closer.

"Listen, listen, do you hear the music?" The others stopped talking about the light in the sky and were quiet. Far away, but coming closer, they heard singing.

Then the whole sky was filled with light. The shepherds saw an angel standing in front of them. The angel said, "Do not be afraid. A Saviour has been born tonight. You will know it is true when you see a baby in a manger."

Then suddenly, there were angels all around the shepherds! The angels sang, "Glory to God in the highest, and on earth, peace to the men who please Him." The angel music was soft, but it seemed to shake the very ground.

The shepherds fell on their knees. They blessed God for letting them see and hear such special things. When it was dark again, they stared at each other. "Was I dreaming?" one asked. No, they knew it was for real. The shepherds gathered the sheep and headed for Bethlehem.

As they neared the village, they noticed the giant star was standing still over a certain hillside. They saw a cave there and noticed people inside. The shepherds went to look. There was the baby the angels had told them about!

They knelt and worshipped Him as King and Saviour. Mary and Joseph watched. Mary knew she would never forget that night.

The Star That Led to the Baby's Cradle

Matthew 2:1-10

A while later, Mary and Joseph had some very important visitors. They were wise men from faraway lands in the east. They had seen the bright star in the night skies. They believed something great had happened. So they travelled a long distance. They went to King Herod in Jerusalem.

"We believe a King of the Jews has been born. We saw His star in the east. We have come to worship Him," they said to Herod.

Herod knew nothing about Jesus' birth. He asked the religious leaders, "Where is the King of the Jews supposed to be born?"

"In Bethlehem," they answered. They knew the answer because that was what the prophets had said many, many years earlier.

"When did the star appear?" Herod asked the visitors. Herod wanted to find out as much as possible about this new king. He did not want anyone taking away his throne. Herod was very cruel and thought of a plan. He ordered the wise men, "Go and honour Him. When you have found Him, come tell me. I want to do the same."

The wise men went to Bethlehem. They followed the star until it stopped. When they went into the house, they saw Baby Jesus in Mary's arms. They smiled and laughed. Their long journey had been worth it. They had found the King!

Gifts for a King

Matthew 2:11-12

The wise men unloaded their camels. They had brought rare and beautiful gifts to the little family. Mary and Joseph's eyes grew round. "Why, these are gifts fit for a king," Mary

whispered to Joseph. He nodded.

One of the wise men bowed before her. "We've travelled a long way. The star showed us where to go. Here is gold for a great King."

The second wise man came up to Mary. "It doesn't happen often that such a large star suddenly appears. That baby will be the greatest of all men." He laid a jar of myrrh at Mary's feet. Myrrh is very special perfume, which could only be worn by very important men.

The third wise man smiled at Mary and Joseph. "This is incense for burning. It will make the air sweet. Incense is pleasing to God. We don't know how, but this King is both man and God."

Mary and Joseph thanked the men. They all bowed their heads in prayer. They thanked God for bringing Jesus into the world.

The night before the visitors were due to go back home, they had a strange dream. In the dream God warned them not to go back and see King Herod. The wise men believed the dream. They went home a different way.

He Will Be Called a Nazarene

Matthew 2:13-23; 13:55; Luke 2:39-40

After the wise men left Mary and Joseph, the family rested. Little Jesus slept and ate, ate and slept. He grew bigger and stronger as the weeks passed.

One night, Joseph had a dream. Like the wise men, he dreamt God was speaking to him. "Wake up. Take the child and His mother. You must run away to Egypt. Stay there until I tell you. King Herod is going to look for the child. He wants to kill Him."

Joseph woke up with a start. The dream seemed so real. He believed it without a doubt. In the past days he had seen how God was in control. Joseph bowed his head. He prayed, "Yes, God. We will do as You say."

Joseph woke Mary up. He told her about the dream. They quickly packed up their few things and put them on the donkey. Joseph gently lifted the sleeping Jesus and put Him into Mary's arms. He led the donkey from the house. They disappeared into the dark night.

Meanwhile, King Herod had waited and waited for the three wise men to return from their visit. When they did not show up, he grew angry. He had wanted to trick them. They had tricked him instead.

"They were supposed to tell me where this king of the Jews is." Herod did not like the idea of another king.

He wanted to be the only king. "Whoever this king of the Jews is, I will kill him! I may not know where he is, but I know he is still just a baby!"

Herod ordered his soldiers to search Bethlehem for the baby king. But when they came to the house, it was empty. Joseph and Mary were safe, and on their way to Egypt.

Several years passed and the wicked King Herod finally died. Joseph, Mary and Jesus spent that time living safely in Egypt.

One night, an angel of the Lord again appeared to Joseph in a dream. "Wake up and take the child and His mother back to Israel," the angel said.

The next morning Joseph told Mary the good news. They were soon on their way back home. They settled in their village, Nazareth. A long, long time ago, one of the prophets had said the Messiah would be called a Nazarene.

In Nazareth Joseph set up shop as a carpenter. People came to him with their broken chairs and tables. Joseph sawed and hammered all day. He carved wood into furniture. As Jesus

grew into a big boy, He often came in the shop to watch Joseph. When Joseph asked Him to help, Jesus would hand Joseph the tools he needed.

In the evenings Joseph and Mary taught Jesus the Jewish history, and about loving God. Joseph and Mary could tell their little boy already knew a great deal about God. The little family learned from each other in those early years when Jesus was a boy.

Joseph and Mary Lose Jesus

Luke 2:41-52

When Jesus was twelve years old, Mary and Joseph took Him to Jerusalem. Because it was time for the Passover feast, the city was full of people.

On the last day of the festival Mary and Joseph left to go home. They both thought Jesus was with the other children who were going back to Nazareth.

After a whole day of travelling, they asked the other children from the group. "Have you seen Jesus?" The children shook their heads.

Mary and Joseph looked at each other. Jesus was still back in Jerusalem! How would they ever find Him? They left the group and hurried back to the city. There they looked everywhere for Him. Mary and Joseph saw many children. None of them was Jesus.

For three days they searched high and low. Mary and Joseph felt desperate. They had lost their precious Son, God's Son. Finally, they went to the temple where the Jewish people worshipped on the Sabbath and holy days.

As they entered, Joseph spotted a group of teachers listening to someone. There, in the middle of the group sat Jesus. He was the one everyone was listening to.

Mary and Joseph pushed their way toward Jesus. When they reached Him, Mary said, "Child, why didn't You try to find us? We've looked everywhere for You. We were so worried."

Jesus said, "Why didn't you know where to look? Of course, you should have known I had to be doing my Father's work."

Jesus meant, that since He was God's Son, he would be in the temple, His Father's house. As they left the temple with Jesus, they heard many people say, "How can such a young boy talk as wisely as He did?"

Jesus returned with His parents to Nazareth. There He was a good boy and did what His parents told Him. These were special years.

Jesus Is Baptized

Matthew 3:1-17; Mark 1:1-11; Luke 3:1-22; John 1:29-34

Jesus had a cousin. He was called John the Baptist. John was the son of Elizabeth, Mary's old friend.

When John grew to be a man, God told him to give the people a special message. "Get ready!" John told them. "Get ready for the One who is coming!"

The crowds sat on the riverbank listening to him. John baptized the people. He told them it showed how God could wash them clean. "Say you're sorry. Start again fresh."

John looked up to see who was next in line. It was Jesus! The two cousins stared at each other.

Jesus went down into the water. When He came out, He was praying. Suddenly, it seemed as though the sky had split in two! God's Holy Spirit had come. It looked like a dove as it hovered over Jesus. This showed all those watching that Jesus had the Holy Spirit in Him.

A great Voice spoke from the sky, "You are My Son. I have always loved You. You have always pleased Me." It was the Voice of God. He was telling the people they should listen to Jesus.

Jesus and His Friend

John 1:19-34

Sometimes when John the Baptist preached, a group of religious leaders

224

would watch him closely. They wanted to know whether John was really a prophet sent from God. "Who is this strange man preaching in the middle of a river?" they asked each other.

The religious leaders asked John, "Who are you?"

John said, "I am not the Christ." John knew that Jesus was the Messiah, or Christ.

"But why are you baptizing then, if you are not the Christ or the Prophet?"

"I baptize in water, but there is One standing in the crowd now. I'm not even good enough to be His slave." The Pharisees looked around. They saw no one who looked important.

A few days later John saw Jesus in the crowd again. He called out, "There is the Lamb of God. He takes away the sin of the world! I've been using water to baptize you with, but there is someone here who will baptize you with God's Spirit! He is the Son of God, but you don't know Him yet!"

When the Pharisees heard John, they grew even more confused and angry. They watched Jesus move through the crowd. "It's bad enough that John has so many people following him. If this Jesus becomes even more popular than John, our problems are bigger than we think." They decided to keep an eye on both John and Jesus.

The Enemy of God Tempts Jesus

Matthew 4:1-12; 14:3-5; Mark 1:12-14; 6:17-20;
Luke 3:19-20; 4:1-13

After Jesus was baptized in the river, He went into the desert to pray. God's enemy met Jesus in the desert. God's enemy, the devil, wanted to spoil God's plans for Jesus. He hates it when people grow close to God.

Jesus was the Son of God. He could have anything He wanted. God's enemy wanted Jesus to choose to use His power in the wrong ways. So God's enemy tempted Jesus.

Jesus was in the desert for forty days and nights. He had not eaten all that time. This was Jesus' way of keeping His thoughts on God alone.

God's enemy knew Jesus was hungry. He first tried to tempt Jesus with food. "If You are the Son of God, tell this stone to become bread."

Jesus knew it was more important to do what God wanted. He answered, "Food isn't the most important thing in life. What's really important is being near to God and doing what He says."

Then God's enemy led Jesus to the top of a high place. He pointed to all the castles and far kingdoms of the world. "If You worship me," God's enemy said, "if You call me king, I will give all these kingdoms to You."

Jesus told him, "I only serve the Lord God,"

Lastly, God's enemy led Jesus to Jerusalem. He set Him on the edge of the temple roof. It was very, very high up. "Jump," God's enemy said. "If God really loves You, He will send His angels to catch You."

"You should not test the Lord your God," Jesus said. "Now go away. I'm not going to do what you want. I've come here to do what God wants!"

When God's enemy left, angels come to take care of Jesus.

When Jesus left the desert He heard that John the Baptist had been put in prison by King Herod. This news made Jesus very sad.

The First Disciples

John 1:35-51

Just before John the Baptist was taken prisoner, he had told two of his men to go and follow Jesus. One man was called Andrew. When he and his friend found Jesus, they started walking behind Him. Jesus turned and said, "What do you want?"

They asked if they could go to where He was staying that evening. They wanted to listen to Him teach. Jesus said yes.

John's followers had learned from John how important it is to listen to the truth. John had said, "One greater than I is coming soon. Follow Him."

As Andrew listened to Jesus, he thought to himself, "I must tell everyone I know that this is the man John was talking about."

Andrew went to find his brother. "Simon!" he called. "Simon, we've found the Messiah! Come, Simon, come and we'll take you to Him."

Simon did not know what to think. When Jesus saw him, He said, "You are Simon the son of John. You will be called Cephas or Peter." The names Cephas and Peter both meant "Rock." This was the first time Jesus met Simon. Because of this meeting, Simon soon came to be called Simon Peter. Later he was called Peter.

The next day Jesus went to Galilee. There he saw a man called Philip. "Follow Me," He said, and Philip did so.

Philip went to a friend called Nathanael. He said, "We've found the One Moses and the prophets spoke about. It's Jesus from Nazareth!"

Nathanael laughed. He said he did not think there were any good people in Nazareth. But when he actually saw Jesus, Jesus said, "I know you, Nathanael. You believe in God. You try very hard to do what He wants. Just now, I know you were sitting under a fig tree, thinking, when Philip called you."

Nathanael was amazed that Jesus

would know what he had been doing. Nathanael said, "I believe. You are the Son of God. You are the King of Israel."

Jesus smiled. "Do you believe so easily? I tell you, you will see greater things than these."

This Is How to Catch Fish

Matthew 4:18-22; Mark 1:16-20; Luke 5:1-11

After Andrew brought Peter to meet Jesus, the two brothers returned home. They were fishermen and needed to take care of their boats and nets.

Peter noticed a huge crowd of people coming toward him. They were being led by Jesus.

Jesus walked right up to Peter. He got into his boat and asked him to pull out a little way from the land. Then Jesus sat down in the boat. He began teaching all the people who lined the shore.

When Jesus had finished speaking, He turned to Peter. "Go out into the deep water and let down your nets for a catch."

Peter said, "Teacher, we worked hard all night and caught nothing. But all right, I will do as You say."

Peter dropped his net overboard. He started to haul it in again and got the surprise of his life. It was full to the bursting point! He called another boat to come and help him. By the time he and the other men had hauled all the fish on board, both boats were ready to sink.

When Peter saw the great catch of fish, he cried, "Oh, yes, You are the Lord! But I'm not a good man at all. Please just leave me alone!"

Jesus told him and Andrew, "Don't be afraid. Follow Me and I will help you become fishers of men." Then Peter and Andrew put down their nets. They landed their boats, which were full of fish, and followed Jesus.

As they walked along the shore, they soon met Peter's partners, two brothers named James and John. Jesus went up to them. "Follow Me," He said. They took one look at Jesus' face, felt their hearts turn over and agreed.

These men became Jesus' closest friends. They followed Him everywhere as He taught the people. They watched and learned from Him. They were Jesus' helpers, His disciples.

There's No More Wine!

John 2:1-11

A few days later, Jesus and His disciples were invited to a wedding in Nathanael's hometown of Cana. It was a big wedding. The party lasted several days. Jesus' mother Mary was there, too.

There were many, many people at the wedding. Food was heaped on tables. There was meat and nuts, rice, cakes and fruit.

All the guests drank a great deal of wine. Halfway through the feast the bridegroom noticed the wine was running out. "Oh no," he thought to

himself. "This is terrible!"

It was the bridegroom's job to make sure there was enough wine. If the wine ran out that meant the party might end early. That was no fun!

Mary saw the bridegroom's problem. She went to Jesus. "They have no wine," she said.

Jesus said, "But why do you ask Me about this now? You know it's not yet time for Me to let people know who I am."

Mary called a servant anyway. She told him to do what Jesus ordered. Jesus told the servant to fill six huge jars with water.

Once the jars were full, He said, "Take out some water now. Bring it to the head waiter." When the head waiter had tasted the wine, he took it to the bridegroom.

"What have you done?" he asked him. "This is the best wine I've ever tasted!" The bridegroom did not know where all the wine had come from, but Mary knew.

230

The Unholy Temple

John 2:13-25

Jesus and His followers travelled to Jerusalem. When they arrived, it was almost time for the Jewish Passover. They went straight to the temple. It was the same place where Mary and Joseph had found Jesus when they lost Him as a boy.

When Jesus arrived at His Father's house this time, He did not like what He saw. Instead of people praying to God and studying the laws of Moses, they were using the temple as a market.

People sold sheep and cows and birds to offer as sacrifices. The temple rang with all the baaing and mooing and shouting. Jesus' disciples looked at Him. They could tell He was upset.

Suddenly, Jesus grabbed a whip. He

232

ran through the courtyard of the
temple. His disciples stood and
watched with open mouths. Jesus ran
back and forth. He drove the animals
and people from the area. "Get out!"
He shouted. "Take these things away!
How dare you turn My Father's house
into a marketplace!"

He turned over the tables of the
moneychangers. Coins splashed all
over the floor. Animals ran in every
direction. People shouted.

When Jesus had finished, He took a
few moments to relax. Then He started
teaching the people who had followed
Him. During the next days of the
Passover feast, He taught people about
God. He also did several miracles.
Many people believed what He said.
They wanted to learn more and
promised they would always follow
Jesus.

233

He Is the Water of Life

John 4:1-26

Jesus and His followers passed through a land called Samaria. The people there, the Samaritans, were long-time enemies of the Jews. No Jew ever wanted to talk to a Samaritan.

All the same, when Jesus arrived at a well in Samaria, He started talking with a Samaritan woman. Jesus was very tired from all the walking. He asked her, "Can you give Me a drink of water?"

She was surprised that a Jew would talk to her. She drew some water out of the well and gave it to Him. "Why do You, who are a Jew, talk to me, a Samaritan?" she asked.

Jesus said, "If you knew the life God could give you, if you knew who I was, you'd be the one asking Me for water. Then I would give you the living water from God. If you drink the water I give, you'll live for ever and never be thirsty again."

This puzzled the Samaritan woman. Water is something we all need in order to keep living. Especially in hot countries like Samaria, water is very precious. It is often hard to find. Jesus said, "Whoever drinks the water I can give will never be thirsty again."

"Oh, I want that!" she cried.

Then Jesus told her to get her husband. When she said she had no husband, Jesus told her all about her life. He even knew how many husbands she had had. "And the man you are living with now is not your husband," He added.

The woman was very confused. How could He know all her secrets? She was scared of Him and tried to change the subject. Jesus knew what she was thinking. He wanted to help her. She said she did not know much about God, but had heard about a

Messiah who would someday come to earth.

Then Jesus said, "The Messiah is already here. You're talking to Him now!"

The Woman at the Well

John 4:27-42

"Who is that woman at the well?"

Jesus' disciples were walking back from the town where He had sent them to get food. When they saw Him talking to the woman they became very upset. "Jesus shouldn't do that. She's a Samaritan. No Jew wants to talk to those people," they said to each other.

When the woman looked at the disciples' angry faces, she thought she had better go home. Jesus had given her a great deal to think about. She left her water pot behind and hurried into town. There she told a group of people, "Come and see a man who told me all about my life! Is it possible? Could this really be the Christ?"

The woman's story made the people very curious. They followed her to the well and met Jesus. They listened to Him teach and felt their hearts and minds open to what He said. "Please, stay with us and tell us some more," they begged.

Jesus' disciples did not like this. They did not want to stay with the Samaritans. But Jesus showed His love for all types of people. He stayed in that city for two days. Many people believed He was the Messiah. Some believed because of the story told by the woman at the well. Most believed for themselves because of what they heard Jesus say. He taught about love and then had spent time with them, even though He was a Jew and they were Samaritans.

"Let us by! Let us through to Jesus!" they called out. When they saw they would never make it through the door, two of the men climbed on top of the roof of the house. The other two threw them ropes so they could haul the stretcher onto the roof.

On the stretcher lay a very sick man. He could not move at all. His four friends had brought him to see Jesus. They knew Jesus could make him better.

The four men began pulling tiles off the roof. They were making a hole! Inside the house, the people listening to Jesus heard a ripping sound above them. They looked up. Then suddenly, dirt and tiles fell on them. The next thing they knew, a stretcher was being lowered through the hole with a sick man strapped onto it!

Jesus saw how hard the man's friends had worked. He told the sick man all the bad things he might have done no longer mattered. He could start again. Jesus said, "Now get up and walk home."

The man did as he was told, just as if he had never been sick. "Glory to God! This really is His Son!" He and his four friends shouted and sang the whole way home.

The Tax Collector Says Yes

Matthew 9:9-13; Mark 2:14-17; Luke 5:27-32
As Jesus was walking down the street he passed a table where a tax collector sat. The Jewish people did not like tax

Four Men on the Roof

Matthew 9:2-8; Mark 2:1-12; Luke 5:18-26
One day while Jesus was teaching inside a friend's house, many, many people came to listen. They crowded around the tiny house. They tried to hear at least a few words of what Jesus was saying.

Four men carrying a stretcher pushed their way through the people.

collectors. They worked for the Romans, who were enemies of the Jews. No one liked the tax collectors because they were such cheaters.

As Jesus passed this tax collector called Matthew, He said, "Follow Me!"

Matthew had already heard about Jesus. He wanted to follow Him, but Matthew was afraid Jesus would say no. Matthew was a tax collector, after all. When Jesus said, "Follow Me," Matthew jumped up from his table. He left behind his books and box of money. Matthew followed Jesus.

A few evenings later, Jesus was eating dinner in Matthew's house. Sitting with Him were more tax collectors and cheaters.

When the religious leaders, saw this, they were not happy. They said to Jesus' followers, "Why does Jesus eat with all these bad people?"

Jesus said, "Do the healthy need a doctor? No, the sick are the ones who need help." Then He told them to think about how it was better to care for people with problems than waste time trying to follow rules which could only hurt people.

This was a new teaching for the religious leaders. They were used to thinking of God's rules as reasons to punish and judge. Jesus told them that God had given them the rules so they would know right from wrong. They were supposed to love and help each other.

Waiting for a Miracle

John 5:1-9

One day Jesus visited a special gate in Jerusalem called Bethesda. Near that gate was a pool with large steps. Many sick people lay on these steps. They were waiting for the water in the pool to move. They believed that sometimes an angel of God came and stirred the water. Whoever was the first one into the water after the angel came, would get better.

When Jesus passed by the pool He saw sick people moaning and groaning. Some lay shrivelled up and dying. One man had been waiting thirty-eight years for the water to move.

Jesus asked this man, "Do you want to get better?"

The sick man answered, "Sir, I have no one to put me into the pool when the water is stirred up."

But that was not what Jesus had asked him. Jesus wanted to know if the man wanted to get better. Still, Jesus said, "Get up. Pick up your bed and walk."

The man felt his body grow warm. All at once, the man was better. He picked up his bed and began to walk!

The Twelve Men Set Apart

Matthew 10:1-23; Mark 3:13-19; Luke 6:12-16

After Jesus had healed many people, He went off by Himself. He climbed up a mountain and prayed. All night long He prayed to God.

When the sun rose, He called His disciples. He chose twelve of them. These men would be His twelve special helpers. They would be the closest to Jesus. They would be the ones to carry on Jesus' work, after He went to heaven.

It was a strange group Jesus chose.

Peter, James and John were the closest to Jesus. They, as well as Andrew, belonged to the same fishing business. Matthew was a tax collector. Simon (another Simon, not Peter) was mostly interested in fighting a war with the Romans. The other men were Philip, Bartholomew, Thomas, another James and Judas Iscariot and a second man named Judas.

After choosing the twelve, Jesus sat them down and gave them special orders. "Go to the Jews and heal the sick, raise the dead, cleanse the lepers, cast out demons. Give freely," Jesus taught them. "Do not try and become rich. Trust in God's care. You will have enough to eat. Things will not always be easy."

Jesus was getting the apostles ready for the job they would do later. These were the men who would spread God's Good News.

True Happiness

Matthew 5:1-12; Luke 6:20-23

Jesus gave a very important talk one day, on a hillside. He wanted to explain some of His teaching. Many, many people followed Him there. The talk Jesus gave is called the Sermon on the Mount.

On that hillside, Jesus taught the people about real happiness. The people noticed He turned everything upside-down. Instead of saying the tough and pushy people would be winners, He said the weak people and ones who depended on God were truly happy. This was something the people had never heard before.

"The most precious people in God's eyes are the poor. The special ones are those who are hurting and gentle. They want very badly to see the right thing done. These are the people who take care of others.

"If anyone hurts you because you believe in Me, then be glad. You will surely be rewarded in heaven," Jesus said.

Do You Know How to Be Salt?

Matthew 5:13-16

The people who heard Jesus were astonished. This was like no teaching they had ever heard before. It made them feel loved and wanted by God.

"You are the salt of the earth," Jesus said.

"But how can we be salt?" they asked each other.

The answer is that ordinary people are the ones who make the world a special place. Mothers and fathers raise their children. The peacemakers try to bring people together. People who work hard then come home and play with their children, all these people stop the world from wasting away. They are just like salt because salt helps keep meat from going bad or wasting. And salt makes food taste extra good. Ordinary people, not the rich or powerful people, can change the "taste" of the world from bad to good.

"You are the light of the world. You cannot hide a city on a hillside," Jesus said. He knew the lights of a city would always be seen a long way off.

No one hides a light under a bucket. That would be a silly waste. So, too, people who follow God in their lives should not be afraid to do the things Jesus says. Every man, woman and child who loves God, can show others what God is like. They do this by loving the people around them.

242

The Treasure Hunt

Matthew 6:19-34; Luke 12:22-32

During the Sermon on the Mount Jesus taught His followers how to search for hidden treasure. "Where your treasure is, that is where your heart will be," He said. What did He mean?

Whatever a person thinks about and dreams about, that is what he or she is most in love with. Do you dream about having more toys, saving more money, running faster? Is there something you want more than anything else in the world?

Jesus taught that treasures like these can all disappear. The place to look for hidden treasure is in heaven. "You cannot love money and love God," Jesus said.

"Don't worry about having enough to eat or drink, or how you will buy new clothes," Jesus taught. Put God first in everything and you will see how everything works out for the best. God is bigger than any problem you

made flowers which are more beautiful than even the best clothes of King Solomon."

God knows what people need. The most important thing is to follow Him, to obey Him, to love others as He does. God takes care of the rest.

How to Build a House

Matthew 7:24-29; Luke 6:46-49

Jesus finished His Sermon on the Mount, "If you change your lives, you are like the wise man who built his house on solid rock."

What happens to a house built on rock? It stays put, no matter if it rains hard or the winds blow.

"Those who hear these words, but do not try to change, will be like the foolish man. He built his house upon the sand," Jesus said.

What happens to a house built on sand? It might be very pretty. As soon as a storm hits, as soon as floods rage, the house is swept away. It will fall with a big crash!

Everyone who has heard this teaching by Jesus has a choice. They can walk away, living as they used to. Or they can act on what they have heard. They can let Jesus' teaching change their lives.

might have. Just be sure to talk to Him about it.

"Look at the birds," Jesus pointed at a flock flying overhead. "Your heavenly Father feeds them. Aren't you worth much more than a bird? Why worry about clothes then? God

A Special Act

Luke 7:36-50

A Pharisee named Simon invited Jesus. for dinner one night. The Pharisees were religious leaders. Many of them did not like Jesus because He taught everyone about God's love.

While Jesus was eating with Simon, a woman came into the house. The guests said, "Look, there's that very bad woman."

The woman came over to Jesus. She knelt down.

"What is she doing?" Simon gasped.

Jesus said nothing. The woman was crying. Tears ran over her face and onto Jesus' feet. Then she wiped His feet dry with her hair.

Still, Jesus said and did nothing. He waited for her to finish. But Simon, the Pharisee, thought to himself, "If

Jesus were really a prophet, He would know what kind of awful woman this is."

Then the woman reached into the folds of her dress. She took out a tiny bottle of very, very expensive perfume. It was the sort of perfume every Jewish woman held on to all her life, saving it for a special day. She poured the rich perfume over Jesus' feet. This meant she thought of Him as her King. The room was filled with the lovely smell.

Simon became more and more upset. Jesus knew what he was thinking. "Simon," He said, "I want to tell you a story.

"There once were two men. One owed a great deal of money to the moneylender. The other owed a little bit of money. When neither could pay back what they owed, the moneylender forgave them both. Now which will love him more?"

Simon said, "The one who owed him the most."

"That's right," Jesus said. "Now look at this woman. When I came into your house, you did not give Me any water so I could clean My feet. She made them wet with her tears and wiped them with her hair.

"You gave Me no kiss of greeting. She has kissed My feet constantly. Do you see? Her sins, which are many, have been forgiven because she had so much faith in Me. The person who is forgiven little, loves little."

Planting Seeds

Matthew 13:1-9; Mark 4:1-9; Luke 8:4-8

While Jesus was teaching, He often told stories like this one.

"There once was a man planting seeds in his field. Some seeds fell beside the road. The birds came and ate them up.

"Other seeds fell on rocky ground, where there was not much soil. Those seeds sprouted up easily enough. Because there was nowhere for their roots to find water, though, they died as soon as it became hot.

"Some seeds fell among the thistles. The weeds choked the grain plants. Other seeds fell on good soil. These plants grew strong and tall. The fruit they grew was thirty to a hundred times more than what was first planted."

Jesus looked at all the people listening. A few nodded. They understood. But many more were shaking their heads. They did not know what Jesus was talking about. So Jesus explained the story.

Planting Seeds in the Right Places

Matthew 13:10-23; Mark 4:10-20; Luke 8:9-15

When Jesus told the story of planting seeds, there were many, including His disciples, who did not know what He meant.

Jesus said His stories were a way of finding out who wanted to follow Him. Those who looked for the real lesson behind the stories were serious about living as Jesus wanted them to. To those who had hardened their

hearts, though, His stories were just so many pretty words.

Jesus told them, "The seeds are the lessons I teach. Some people hear the word of God. Sometimes they choose to ignore what they have heard. Then God's enemy, like the birds in the story, steals away what little truth they did manage to learn. These are like the seeds planted by the roadside.

"The seeds planted in rocky places are the people who hear with joy what I teach. They try for a little while to follow Me. It does not take much, just a few problems, before they go back to their old ways. The seeds sown with the thistles are the people who hear the word. They also know what I've taught. But then they let the problems of daily living choke the new life. They worry and want to make more money. So nothing comes from the lessons they learned.

"Lastly, there are the seeds which are planted on good ground. They are the people who listen and practice what they have learned from My stories. They tell God they are sorry for what they have done. They try their hardest to change. These people will teach others about following Me. They will teach by saying, as well as doing."

Jesus taught that anyone who believes in Him can choose where to plant the seed of truth. Will you plant the lessons you have learned in good ground or rocky ground?

The Difference between Wheat and Weeds

Matthew 13:24-30, 36-43

Jesus told His disciples another story, again it had to do with planting seeds.

"The kingdom of heaven is like a man who planted good seed in his field. Then his enemy came and planted weeds together with the wheat."

"When the wheat sprang up, the weeds grew as well. The farmer's workers asked if they should pull up the weeds. 'No, because then you might pull up the young wheat with it,' the farmer said. 'Wait until it is time for the harvest. Then gather the weeds and we will burn them. After that we can harvest the wheat.'"

Then Jesus explained. "The one who planted the good seed is the Son of Man. The field is the world. The wheat plants are those who follow Me. The weeds are those who will not follow Me. Instead they keep on being selfish and hurting other people. The enemy is the devil. The harvest is the end of the world."

Mustard Seed and Yeast

Matthew 13:31-35; Mark 4:30-34; Luke 13:18-21

Jesus' disciples asked Him about the kingdom of God. They knew anyone could belong to this kingdom as soon as they chose to follow Jesus. They knew God was the King, but what was it like?

Jesus told them the kingdom of heaven was like a mustard seed. That is the tiniest of the tiny seeds. Once a mustard seed starts sending down roots, it grows and grows into a tall tree. Mustard trees are often the biggest trees in the garden. Birds love to build their nests in mustard trees.

Jesus used another story to teach the same lesson. "The kingdom of God is like a small bit of yeast which a woman puts into flour." That little pinch of yeast has the power to turn a lump of baked flour into a loaf of bread.

Both stories showed that small beginnings in the kingdom of God can grow in great ways. Even if all a person does is whisper a soft, "Yes Jesus, I believe," that small beginning can be the start of a truly great faith.

Jesus used stories when He taught the people. That way they could picture what He was talking about. Afterwards He explained the stories to His disciples. He wanted them to learn and grow wiser, understanding more and more.

251

The Storm

Matthew 8:18, 23-25; Mark 4:35-38; Luke 8:22-24

At the end of a day spent healing the sick, Jesus pointed to a nearby boat. He told His disciples, "Come with Me. We will cross to the other side." It was His only chance of getting away from the crowds. Jesus was tired. He needed to rest.

At first the water was calm. A few of the disciples looked up at the sky.

"This should be an easy boat ride," one said.

"Don't count on it. You know how this sea can turn wild. For now it does look calm," said another. The disciples moved off to different parts of the boat.

It only seemed like a few moments later when they felt the boat nearly go over. They must be caught in the middle of a storm. All at once, they felt afraid.

One ran to grab hold of the rudder. The wind kept changing. Several times men slipped. They were able to grab onto the side. This kept them from being swept overboard by the huge waves.

Waves broke over both sides of the boat at once. Men scurried back and forth. The skipper wrestled with the rudder. The boat tilted madly from one side to the other. The men felt helpless.

253

They looked at each other. "We have to get Jesus!" When they saw Him asleep on a cushion, they woke Jesus up.

"Teacher! The sea is wild. This is a terrible storm! We'll never reach the other side in one piece. Save us!"

Jesus looked from one troubled face to the other, then He got up. Jesus spread His arms wide. The wind blew hair into His face. His voice boomed, "Be still!"

The Other Side

Matthew 8:26-27; Mark 4:39-41; Luke 8:25

As soon as Jesus called out, "Quiet! Be still!" the wind calmed. The water flattened. Peter ran to the edge of the deck. He looked overboard. He saw his reflection mirrored in the dark sea. He ran back to Jesus and fell on his knees in relief.

Jesus said, "Why don't you have more faith? There's no reason to be afraid when you're with Me." He walked to the other end of the boat.

No one dared speak out loud. An eerie silence hung over them all. They were astonished and afraid.

"What kind of man is this that we are following? Why, even the wind and the waves obey him." Amazed, they kept asking each other this question.

255

The Wild Man in the Graveyard

Matthew 8:28-34; Mark 5:1-20; Luke 8:26-39

When Jesus and his disciples landed their boat, they saw something very strange. There was a man who had evil spirits living inside him.

He was not in control of himself anymore. He had no clothes on. His hands and feet were bloody from wearing chains. He was dirty and could not speak for himself. He lived in graveyards and wandered about in the mountains like a wild man.

When he saw Jesus, he ran and fell on his knees in front of Him. Jesus could tell that the man was not in his right mind. He said, "Come out of this man, evil spirits!"

A herd of pigs grazed nearby. Jesus commanded the spirits to leave the man and go into the pigs. The evil

256

spirits obeyed. As soon as they entered the pigs, the pigs ran over a cliff. They fell all the way down, into the sea.

The men who had been watching over the pigs hurried back to town. When all the people came to see what had happened, they saw the crazy man sitting quietly at Jesus' feet. He was dressed and in his right mind again.

The people grew afraid of the power of Jesus. They begged Him to go back where He had come from.

When He and His disciples climbed back in the boat, the healed man begged to go with Him. "No," Jesus told him, "go home and tell how much the Lord has done for you."

So the man told people in all the nearby towns how Jesus had made him better. And all the people were amazed.

More People Are Healed

Matthew 9:27-31

People who were blind in the days of Jesus had no chance of living a normal life. There were no braille books, which can be read by feeling bumps on pages. There were no guide dogs, which can help a blind person find his or her way through the streets. Blind people in Jesus' time had no choice but to beg for a living. There was no way they could find work. They were helpless.

Everywhere Jesus went, people followed Him who were hurting in mind and body. They begged Jesus to make them better. One day there were two blind men following Jesus. "Have mercy on us, Son of David!" they called out.

Jesus went into a friend's house. The two men followed. There, He turned and asked them, "Do you really think I can make you see again?"

The two men were friends. They had both heard the stories of Jesus healing people. They believed He was the Messiah. They had stumbled along the roads, bumping up against people as they followed Jesus. Now they were alone with Him. "Yes, Lord," they said.

Jesus reached out His hands and touched their eyes. He said, "What you believe can happen, really will. Just keep on believing."

Suddenly, the men saw lights and colours. Then the shifting blurs became real things. They cried out as they saw Jesus' face smiling at them. Where there had been darkness, now there was light!

The men were so happy they went out and told the news to everyone they met.

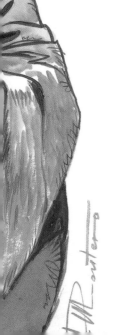

259

The Weak King

Matthew 14:1-12; Mark 6:14-29

As Jesus travelled and taught, His dear friend John the Baptist was still locked up in prison. King Herod had put him there. This was because John had told him he should not have married his brother's wife.

This woman was called Herodias. She hated John. She wanted John the Baptist dead. If it had not been for Herodias, John would have been free.

On King Herod's birthday he held a big party. He invited all his friends, family, counsellors, generals and other important people who served him. The palace was full of people laughing and drinking and eating.

The musicians started playing a strange and lovely song. Everyone turned to watch a beautiful young woman start dancing. Her feet hardly touched the floor. She was more graceful than any dancer they had ever seen.

King Herod smiled. "That is the daughter of my wife, Herodias," he said. "Nobody else can dance like this."

Slowly but surely, the girl made her way over to Herod's table. She danced right in front of him. With a last twirl and toss of her head, she knelt before Herod.

The king felt even more drunk when he looked into her eyes. He said, "Ask me for anything you want and I'll give it to you." Then he promised with an oath which could not be broken.

The girl ran off to her mother, Herodias. She said, "What will I ask for?"

Herodias smiled wickedly. "Ask for the head of John the Baptist on a tray."

When the girl returned to the king and told him her request, the king was very upset. "John is a good man, how can I possibly have him killed?" he thought to himself. He looked around. All the important people were watching him. Herod felt weak. "Very well," he told a guard. "Bring me John's head on a tray."

When John's disciples and friends heard that John was dead, they went to the prison. They claimed John's body so they could bury it. They went and told Jesus about John's death. When Jesus heard that His closest of friends was dead, He grew very, very sad.

To a Quiet Place

Matthew 14:13; Mark 6:30-33; Luke 9:10; John 6:1-3

A few days after Jesus heard about
John the Baptist's death, He had to go
out and help a huge crowd of people.
He did not even have time to eat. He
felt so very sad because His cousin
John was dead. The more He heard
the crowds call out for Him, the more
weary He felt.

So Jesus called Peter. He pointed to
a boat, beached nearby. "I must be
alone. Let's go away and rest a while."

Jesus and His disciples went in the
boat by themselves to a lonely place.
There they prayed for each other. God
made them stronger and more sure of
what they were doing.

But the crowd knew that Jesus had gone away somewhere. They tried to find out where. It did not take long before even more people crowded the shores of the lake. They watched for the boat. When they saw Jesus' boat heading back to shore, a great shout went up. People from many cities ran up and down the beach.

Teaching Thousands

Matthew 14:14-15; Mark 6:34-36; Luke 9:11-12

When the boat carrying Jesus and His disciples finally landed, many of the people waded out to meet it. "Jesus! Jesus!" they called to Him.

All that afternoon He told them stories. He taught about the love of God. The crowd was so huge, it stretched out for miles. The sun shone and birds sang. It was a beautiful day. The people sat on the sand and the grass. They listened and watched as Jesus healed the sick and prayed for them. In some ways it felt just like a big picnic.

But there was one thing missing. There is always food at a picnic. As the afternoon wore on, more and more of the people complained about how hungry they were. Finally, in the evening, the disciples came to Jesus. They said He should send the people home so they could get something to eat. "At least let them go and find some food in the nearby villages," they said.

Food for the Hungry

Matthew 14:16-18; Mark 6:37-38; Luke 9:13; John 6:4-9

Jesus looked at all the thousands of people around Him. The people were excited by all they had learned that day. He did not want to end the teaching quite yet. He said to Philip, "Where can we buy enough food for all these people?"

Philip stared at Jesus. "Why, it would take eight months of work to pay for all the food this crowd would eat! But even then they would only get a few pieces of bread each."

Then Andrew, Peter's brother, came up to Jesus. "There is a little boy here. He has five loaves of bread and two fish. But that's not much, is it?"

Jesus' disciples did not know it, but He had asked them to feed the people for a reason. He was trying to teach them yet one more lesson about having faith in God's love.

The Boy Whose Lunch Fed Thousands

Matthew 14:19-21; Mark 6:39-44; Luke 9:14-17; John 6:10-14

Jesus told the people to sit in small groups. Then He thanked the little boy who had given his bread and fish. Jesus held up the five loaves and two fish.

Everyone stopped talking. Jesus looked up. He thanked God for giving them something to eat. He blessed the food and broke the loaves. Then He passed it to the disciples so they could give it to the people.

That is when something very special happened! Jesus gave more bread and more bread and more bread to the disciples. When the disciples' baskets were empty, they came back for more. Jesus put even more bread and fish in the baskets. More and more and more! Until finally, all the thousands and thousands and thousands of men, women and little children had eaten enough.

The disciples collected the crusts and bones and fish heads and other scraps left over from the meal. When they had finished, there were twelve baskets of leftovers! It was a miracle!

Jesus Walks on Water

Matthew 14:22-27; Mark 6:45-52; John 6:15-21

After Jesus had fed the thousands, He told His disciples to climb back into the boat. "Go ahead of Me to the other side."

Then he turned to the crowds. "Calm down, calm down." They were shouting and chanting His name. After all, He had found a way to give them free food. But Jesus said, "Now go on home." Even though there were thousands and thousands of them, the people listened.

After they were gone, Jesus went off by Himself. He climbed a nearby mountain and prayed until it grew dark.

Meanwhile, the disciples had been trying to cross to the other side of the lake. This was not easy to do in the dark. The wind had changed and a storm had started.

In the darkest part of the night, the storm went wild. Wind came from all directions at once. They were still about three or four miles from shore when John yelled. "I see a ghost! Something is walking on water!" But of course, it was not a ghost. The person they saw passing by the boat was Jesus.

Jesus said, "Don't be afraid! It's just Me, Jesus!" The disciples huddled in the far corner of the boat. They were too afraid to believe Him.

Peter Walks on Water

Matthew 14:28-33

The wind roared. The waves formed walls around the boat. Of the little group of scared men, one man stood up. It was Peter. "It's Jesus!" he said to the others. Then he took a step toward the side of the boat and took a closer look.

The Lord's feet barely touched the water. But He did not sink. Jesus took a step toward the boat. Peter called out, "Lord, if it is You, command me to come to You on the water."

Jesus said, "Come!"

Peter put one foot over the side. It went down, down, down, then stopped. Then he swung his second leg over and stood up. He did not sink!

He took a step. Then another and another, all the time watching the face of Jesus. Peter was walking on water!

But after a few steps, he heard the wind howling. And he looked down. Instead of looking at Jesus and trusting in Him, Peter grew afraid. He looked at the waves around him. "How can I walk on water?," he wondered. As soon as Peter started doubting, Peter began to sink. "Help! Lord, save me!" he cried out.

Jesus reached out His hand. He grabbed Peter. Jesus said, "Oh Peter, Peter! Where is your faith? Why did you doubt?"

Jesus and Peter climbed back into the boat. Once they were safe on board, the wind suddenly stopped. The disciples were astounded. They fell to their knees and worshipped Jesus. Not only had they watched Peter walk on water, but Jesus controlled even the very wind and sea.

The Faith of a Foreigner

Matthew 15:21-28; Mark 7:24-30

God's plan for Jesus at that time was that He should first try and teach the people of Israel. Later the good news of God's love would be made known to everyone else in the world.

Many Jews chose not to believe Jesus. There were other people who did believe Jesus was the Son of God. One of them was a woman with a very sick little girl.

This woman went to the house where Jesus was staying. She knelt at

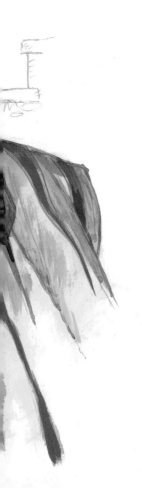

His feet. She cried out, "Please help me! My daughter is very sick!

Jesus did not say a word. He did this to find out how much she believed in Him.

In the same way, God sometimes does not answer our prayers right away. He does not say yes and He does not say no. He says wait. And that is when our faith is built up and made stronger, just like muscles when we exercise.

Another reason Jesus remained silent was because the woman was not a Jew. It was not yet time for Him to teach and heal the non-Jews. It was hard for Jesus to turn away from the woman.

"Please, Lord! Please, make my little girl better!"

His disciples said, "Send her away. She's making too much noise."

"Right now I am only supposed to take care of the Jews," Jesus told the woman. "It is not good to take bread from God's children and throw it to the dogs."

But she said, "Yes, Lord. Yet even the dogs feed on the crumbs which fall from the master's table."

When Jesus heard her answer, He felt His heart burn with love. "Woman, your faith is great. Because of this answer, your daughter is normal again. Go on home."

The woman did as Jesus told her. Once home, she found her little girl asleep in bed. And she was all better!

A Blind Man Healed at Bethsaida

Mark 8:22-26

Jesus went to a little village called Bethsaida. There, a group of people brought a blind man to Him. "Please, Teacher, please touch our friend and make him better."

Jesus took the blind man by the hand. He led him out of the village.

The blind man did not know what to think as he followed Jesus. He could feel Jesus' hand in his own, and it was rough. The blind man's friends had told him, "Jesus has healed others, He can heal you."

Jesus stopped. The blind man felt Jesus take His hand away. Then He heard Him spit. The next thing he knew, he felt the wet warmth of both Jesus' hands against his eyes.

When Jesus took His hands away from the man, He asked him, "Do you see anything?"

The man looked up. He moved his head from side to side. "I see men, but they are like trees, just moving shapes."

Then Jesus laid His hands on the man's eyes again. The man squinted. He began to see everything clearly. Colours danced and the smiles of his friends greeted him. "I can see! I can see!" he shouted to them. They all gathered around him and hugged him, thanking Jesus.

The Rock Man

Matthew 16:13-19; Mark 8:27-29; Luke 9:18-20

Jesus brought His disciples to a quiet place north of Lake Galilee. There, He turned to them and asked a very important question. "Who do people say that I am?"

"Some say John the Baptist, come back to life. To some, You're Elijah. Others say Jeremiah or one of the prophets."

Jesus said to them, "But who do you say that I am?"

Then Peter stepped forward. He felt pushed from inside his heart to answer, "You are the Christ, the Son of the living God."

Jesus said to him, "You are very special and blessed, Peter. The only way you could have known that was if My Father in heaven had shown it to you."

Jesus laid His hands on His friend's shoulders. "Remember your name Peter," He said.

Peter means "Rock," the large, sturdy kind of rock upon which houses are built. The reason for this name became clear when Jesus said, "My Church will be made up of people like you. They know that I am the Christ sent from God. You are the Rock who will help build this Church."

In the same way, all who believe in Jesus have built their lives on the strong "rock" of Jesus' truth. The house built on rock cannot be blown away by the storm.

273

Moses and Elijah

Matthew 17:1-9; Mark 9:2-10; Luke 9:28-36

Six days after this, Jesus called Peter and the two brothers James and John. He had a big surprise for them! Together they climbed a nearby mountain to pray. When they reached the top, Peter, James and John lay down on the ground to rest.

While they were falling asleep, Jesus began to pray. Suddenly, He looked very different! Light seemed to beam from Jesus' face. His clothing became dazzling white and flashed like lightning.

Then, as if out of nowhere, two men appeared. There was Moses, the man who had led the people of Israel out of Egypt and received the Ten Commandments from God. And there was Elijah, the greatest of all the prophets! Moses had died about 1,500 years earlier. Elijah had disappeared into heaven almost a thousand years before. Now they had left heaven for a few moments and come back to earth to talk with Jesus.

The three disciples woke up with a start. "What has happened?" they gasped. They heard Jesus talking about the time coming soon when He would go to Jerusalem and then leave them.

Peter was scared. He said, "Teacher, this is too good to be true. Let's make three tents, one for You, one for Moses and one for Elijah." He wanted the two important men to stay longer.

But just then, a bright cloud came over the hill. It was like a white fog swirling mist around their feet. A Voice came out of the cloud, "This is My Son, My chosen One. Listen to Him!"

The disciples were terrified. They fell face down onto the ground.

When the Voice stopped, Jesus came to them and said, "It's all right. You can get up now. There's no reason to be afraid."

Slowly, they opened their eyes. It was as if nothing had happened.

The Children Come First

Matthew 18:1-14; Mark 9:33-37; Luke 9:46-48

The disciples were walking with Jesus and whispering to each other. "I wonder which one of us is the greatest of all?" Some said it was Peter. Others thought John was the most important disciple. They began to argue about it.

When they asked Jesus what He thought, Jesus did not answer right away. There was a child playing nearby. Jesus called the child over and put him on His knee. "Do you see this little one?" He asked. "Anybody who can become like a child, trusting and humble, that person will become the greatest in the kingdom of heaven.

"And whoever takes care of a child and teaches him or her about Me, has also welcomed Me. But people who hurt a child, or teach him or her not to trust in Me, will be in terrible trouble. It would be better for them if a huge stone were tied around their neck and someone threw them into the water!"

His friends shivered at the thought. They looked at the little child on Jesus' lap. How could a child be so important, they wondered.

Jesus said, "Take care of the children and love them the same way a shepherd loves his sheep. A shepherd searches all night just to find the one missing sheep. Every single child is so very precious to God. He loves them all."

Not Alone

Matthew 18:15-20

Jesus' disciples asked, "What if somebody cheats us? What if someone does something really wrong?"

Jesus told them that if someone hurts them, they should first go to that person alone. They should gently see if they can somehow help make things right again. "If that does not work, then take friends with you," He said. Only when the person refuses to admit he is wrong, should you report him.

The Lord smiled His gentle, strong smile. "Remember, I'm always going to be with you. Whenever two or more of you gather together, I'll be listening. I will be right there, in the same room with you, listening to your prayers."

That is why we are never alone. Even though we cannot see Jesus. He is by our side, watching over us.

The Healed Leper

Luke 17:11-16

As Jesus passed through a certain village, ten lepers waited to meet Him. They had heard He might come that way. They hoped that He might heal them.

Because they were lepers, they were not allowed to stand near the road. From a distance they called out, "Jesus! Teacher! Have mercy on us!" They wore hoods over their heads and scarves across their faces. This was so no one would have to look at the awful sores which made them lepers. They begged Jesus to heal them.

Jesus pointed back to the town. "Go and show yourselves to the priests." This was another way of telling the lepers they were healed! Only people who had been healed were supposed to go to the priests.

The men did as Jesus told them. As they walked toward the temple to see the priests, they felt a strange thing happening. Blood tingled through their arms and legs. A strange warmth went up and down their backs. One man pulled his sleeve up and saw the skin growing back healthy.

He shouted, "Praise God! Praise the Lord God Almighty! I've been healed! I'm all better!"

Then he turned around. As fast as he could, he ran straight back to where Jesus was preaching. He fell at Jesus' feet and grabbed hold of them. "Thank You, oh thank You!" he said.

Why Not Say Thank You?

Luke 17:17-19

Jesus looked at the man who was singing out his thanks to God. He said, "But weren't there ten who were healed? Where are the other nine?" Then Jesus told him, "You can go now. Your faith has saved you and made you better."

Why did only one man return? It could be that the other nine did not come back and say thank you for the same reasons people do not thank God today.

Perhaps one leper simply forgot to say thank you. Another may have been too shy. Maybe one was too proud.

Perhaps another leper was so excited about being healed, he lost his way and could not find Jesus again. It could be one was too busy. There was a lot of living to catch up on.

One leper may not have come back to say thank you because the priest told him he did not have to. This man always did what others told him, without thinking for himself. The seventh leper may not have said thank you because he did not understand what had happened to him. The eighth leper may not have gone back to see Jesus because he simply saw no reason to. He had never said thank you to anyone for anything.

Perhaps the last leper wandered away so happy, he hardly noticed where he was going. Only one leper of the ten saw how Jesus heals the whole person. As happens so often, the others took the gift God gave them for granted. God often gives us what we need. How often do we thank Him?

A Second Chance

John 8:1-11

Jesus went back to Jerusalem. There he taught in the temple. One morning, the religious leaders dragged a woman before Him. She sobbed with fear. The men threw her at Jesus' feet.

"Teacher," they said, "this woman was found together with a man. He was not her husband. The laws Moses gave us say we should throw stones at her until she dies. What do You say?"

The woman did not even lift her head. She and the man she had been with had done a very bad thing. By loving someone other than their own husband and wife, they had hurt their own marriages.

Jesus bent down and wrote in the dust. "Well?" the religious leaders asked. "What do You think we should do with her?"

Jesus stood up. He said, "Let the person who has never done anything wrong be the first to throw a stone at her." Jesus was teaching them not to judge.

The people looked at each other. Everybody knew they had all done something wrong. After all, nobody is perfect. So one by one, the people shuffled away. The old people in the crowd left first. Then the young men left. Finally even the religious leaders turned and walked away. No one said a word. In the end, Jesus was left alone with the woman. She knelt in the dust beside Him.

"Woman," Jesus said, "has no one punished you?"

She raised her head and looked around. Her hair was tangled. "No one, Lord," she mumbled.

Jesus said, "Then I will not punish you, either. But make sure you never do this again. Be sorry. Go back to your husband and start again."

The woman began to cry. But this time the tears were those of joy, rather than fear.

The Good Samaritan

Luke 10:25-37

One day while Jesus was preaching, a man asked Him a question. This man had spent many years studying God's law. He said, "Teacher, what must I do to get to heaven?"

Jesus answered, "What does God's law say? What do you think?"

The man answered, "Love God and others as much as I love myself." When Jesus told him he was right, the man asked, "But what others? Who is my neighbour? Who are the others I should be loving?"

Jesus explained by telling this story. "There once was a man walking from Jerusalem to Jericho. He was alone. The road he followed was rocky, with many twists and turns. Suddenly, robbers jumped out of nowhere. They attacked the man! They beat him up and stole everything he had, even his clothes.

"The man lay bleeding to death on the side of the road. Along came a priest. When he saw the man, he was shocked. He stood and stared. The man could barely raise his head to beg for help. The priest only backed away. He tried not to look. He passed by him as quickly as he could.

"The man lay in the dirt, moaning. Along came a religious leader, one who preached the laws of Moses. He saw the man, all covered in blood and dirt and making funny noises in the ditch. He thought, 'Oh, he looks

terrible. I wouldn't ever want to touch him. Besides, I'm sure he's no one I know.' So this man passed him by, as well.

"Then a Samaritan came walking along the road. The man who lay in the dirt was a Jew. Samaritans and Jews had been enemies for hundreds of years. Still, the Samaritan came over to him. Very gently, he lifted the man's head and brushed the dust out of his mouth. He took some water and cleaned the man's eyes and gave him something to drink. He put wine on his wounds to clean them and oil to make them heal quickly. Then he carried the man and put him onto his donkey. He brought him into town.

"There, the Samaritan gave some money to an innkeeper. He said, 'Put him in a clean bed. Spend whatever you need to take good care of him until he is strong again.' "

"Now tell Me," Jesus added. "Which of these three men was a true neighbour to the man who was robbed?"

The expert in Jewish law did not need to think very long. He said, "The one who helped him of course."

Jesus then told him, "Then go and do just the same."

Those who heard Jesus tell this story knew which people Jesus wanted His followers to love. The "others" were not just friends. Jesus wants His followers to love everybody, especially strangers and those in need.

Martha and Mary

Luke 10:38-42

Jesus wants to be a Friend to good people and bad, stranger and disciple. While Jesus walked the earth He had three best friends besides His disciples. They were sisters, Martha and Mary, and their brother, Lazarus. They opened their home to Jesus. They asked Him to make it His own. As Jesus travelled, He often stayed with Martha, Mary and Lazarus. It was a good place to rest and get away from all the crowds.

During one of His visits, Martha learned a very important lesson. Jesus was relaxing in the main room. He was talking to Mary. Her sister Martha was very excited that Jesus was visiting them. She wanted everything to be just right. She busied herself cooking and cleaning.

"I want this to be a perfect evening," she told herself. There was only one problem. Martha could not possibly do all the work by herself.

She rushed about, gathering herbs and vegetables from the garden, cleaning and cooking.

When Martha looked over from the kitchen, she noticed her sister Mary doing nothing at all. Mary sat at Jesus' feet, listening to all that He said. "Why, she's not even helping a little," Martha thought. "And there's still so much to do!"

Just then, Jesus looked up at Martha. He rose and crossed the room. "Lord," she said, "don't You care that my sister has left me to do all the serving alone? Please tell her to help me."

But Jesus answered, "Martha, Martha, you are worried and bothered about so many things. Only a few things are worth it. Really only one. Mary wants to hear what I teach. That's a good thing and shouldn't be taken away from her. Why don't you do the same?"

Martha looked at Him. All of a sudden, she relaxed. She felt the tight muscles untie their knots. Her face even showed a smile in place of the frowns she had worn all morning. She nodded and followed Jesus back into the room. There she settled onto the floor, next to her sister. Together they listened to the words of Jesus.

From then on, Martha made sure she never made working for Jesus more important than getting to know Him better. It is a lesson all followers of Jesus should remember.

The Good Shepherd

John 10:1-21

Many people wondered, "Who is Jesus? Where did He come from?" They kept asking the same questions over and over again. Jesus knew this and gave them His answer.

"I am the Good Shepherd." Then He painted a word picture for them.

That way they would know why He had called Himself the Good Shepherd.

"I am the gate for the sheep." The shepherd stands at the gate to the pasture. He knows which sheep are his own and lets his sheep pass through the gate. He keeps away all the wild animals who would hurt his animals.

286

"The good shepherd does everything he can to take care of his sheep. He would even die to save them. Because the sheep are his, he does not run away when a wolf comes. He never leaves his sheep to be destroyed. That's what someone who is just hired for the job might do.

"I am the Good Shepherd. I know My sheep and My sheep know Me. I lay down My life for the sheep. I lay down My life so I can take it up again. This is something the Father lets Me do."

Many of the people felt good when they heard Jesus say that. They wanted to believe in Him as their very own Good Shepherd.

288

Lazarus Lives

John 11:1-46

A little later Jesus heard that His friend Lazarus was very sick. Jesus waited a few days before He went to visit him. When He and His disciples did arrive at Martha and Mary's house, Lazarus had already died.

Martha said, "Lord, if You had been here, my brother wouldn't have died. Even now I know that whatever You ask of God, He gives You."

Jesus told her that Lazarus would rise again. But Martha did not understand what He meant. Jesus said, "The person who believes in Me will never die."

When Mary saw Jesus, she fell at His feet. "Lord, if You had been here, he would not have died." She cried and cried. Each tear dropped gently in the dust.

When Jesus saw how upset everyone was, He wept.

"Where have you laid him?" He asked. They led Him toward a cave which was closed off. "Take the stone away."

Once the cave was opened, Jesus gave thanks to God. Then He shouted in a loud voice, "Lazarus, come out!"

Suddenly, a strange shape hobbled out of the cave. He was all covered with bandages and cloths. "Unbind him and let him go," Jesus said.

Mary and Martha rushed forward. They hardly dared to hope that inside the white cloths, Lazarus could be alive. When they had unwrapped him the crowd cried out. There was even more weeping than before. It was Lazarus! And he was alive! The three thanked Jesus.

The Lost Sheep and the Lost Coin

Luke 15:1-10

The price of following Jesus is high. But the value of every single person in God's eyes is even higher. God treasures every child, every man and every woman. He would like nothing better than that each person turn to Him and start his or her life again.

The religious leaders did not like the type of people who followed Jesus. Because of this, Jesus told two stories about how valuable these people are to God. The first story was about a lost sheep.

Jesus asked, "If you had a hundred sheep and lost one of them, wouldn't you go after the one which was lost? And when that sheep was found, wouldn't you carry it back to the flock? Wouldn't you call your friends together? 'I've found my sheep which was lost!' you would shout.

"In the same way, there will be more joy in heaven over one sinner who says, 'I'm sorry,' than over ninety-nine people who think they are so good they don't need God's help."

Heaven is filled with the angels' songs of joy whenever one person comes back to God.

The second story was about a woman who had a set of ten coins. She lost one coin, which was worth an entire day's work. Jesus asked, "If a woman loses one of these silver coins, she will search the house. She will sweep and look under the bed and carpets until she finds it.

"And when she has found it, she will call together her friends and say 'Be happy with me! I finally found the lost coin!'

"In the same way, the angels smile and sing whenever one person says he or she believes in God and wants to live a better life with Jesus' help."

The people were amazed at what Jesus told them. It meant even the bad people, especially the bad people, were welcome in heaven. If they only said they were sorry, God would welcome them back and give them the strength to start again. Jesus was showing them the way into God's very own kingdom. This is the way of loving God and loving others.

The Loving Father

Luke 15:11-19

Jesus told the people a story about a man who had two sons. He said, "One day, the younger son went to his father. He said, 'Father, give me the money which would be mine when you die. I want it today.' The father did not think it was a good idea. He finally agreed. A few days after he got the money, the younger son left home.

"He travelled a long way until he came to a faraway country. There he wasted all his money getting drunk and having wild parties. When his money ran out, he was left with nothing at all. He could not even buy food.

"This younger son went from house to house. He begged for scraps. Finally he ended up working on a farm, feeding pigs. He was so hungry, he wished he could eat with the pigs.

"Before long, this son thought to himself, 'All of my father's workers have more than enough to eat. Yet here I am, starving to death! I must go home and say I'm sorry to my father.' So the younger son left the pigs and headed home."

Coming Home

Luke 15:20-32

As Jesus told the story about the boy who had left home, He hoped the people would learn the lesson of the story. God will forgive anybody and everybody, as long as they are sorry. Anyone who is willing can start fresh again.

Jesus told the rest of the story. "The young man did not know that his father had been watching for him every day since he ran away from home. 'Please let him come home today,' the father had prayed while he stared down the road.

"On this very special day, the son was still a long way off when his father saw him. He shouted, 'There he is! It's him! My son has come home!' He ran down the road and hugged his son.

"But the son hung his head. 'Father,

292

I've been so bad. I don't deserve to be called your son. I lost all my money and. . . .'

"But the father did not let him finish. He ordered his slaves, 'Quickly, bring out the best robe and put it on him. Put a ring on his hand and get him some proper shoes. Kill the calf we were saving for a feast! Let's have a party! My son was dead, and now he lives. He was lost and has been found!'

"The younger son cried for joy when he saw how his father loved him. He was so relieved. Before long, there was a great feast. All of his father's servants and friends joined in the party.

"The older son, though, was not so happy when he came home from working in the fields. He heard music and laughter. He asked a servant why there was a party. When he heard what had happened, he became angry. His father tried to explain. But the older son turned away.

" 'This is just not fair,' he said. 'For so many years I've been the perfect son. I work hard for you. Yet you never so much as gave me a fat goat so I could have a party with my friends. But when this other son wastes your money, you give him everything.'

" 'But you're also my son,' the father said. 'Everything I have belongs to you. Don't you see? This brother of yours was dead and now he's alive. He was lost and has been rescued!' "

293

Money Lovers

Luke 16:10-14

The religious leaders did not like Jesus' teaching about love and forgiveness. Most of them only cared about their money and power.

Jesus said, "You can't live for money and try to please God at the same time. You shouldn't love money and things more than God.

"If people are honest about money matters, it shows they can be trusted. A person who is honest with his money can also be trusted with bigger things, like taking care of people."

Jesus showed the Pharisees they must choose between their love of money and their love of God. Which should come first?

The Rich Man and Lazarus

Luke 16:19-31

Jesus told another story to the people, about the right and wrong ways of living. "There once were two men. One was very rich. The other was very poor. He was named Lazarus. Lazarus was ugly and covered with red sores. He could do nothing but lie on the ground and beg in front of the rich man's gate. He begged for any crumbs which might be left over from the rich man's meals. The dogs used to come and lick his sores.

"But the rich man paid no attention to poor and needy people like Lazarus. He lived selfishly. He wore fine clothes, spent great amounts of money, went to parties and grew fat.

"When Lazarus finally died, the angels came and carried him away. They laid him in Abraham's arms. There he felt no more pain. He was never hungry again.

"But when the rich man died, he was sent to the place where evil people belong. There he suffered terribly. From where he was, the rich man could look up and see Abraham far away, with Lazarus by his side.

" 'Father Abraham!' the rich man called out. 'Have pity on me, please! Send Lazarus with just a little water so I can cool off my tongue! I'm so thirsty here!'

"But Abraham said, 'Don't you remember? During your life you had so many good things, while Lazarus had nothing! Now you're being punished.'

"The rich man said, 'Well, could you send Lazarus to warn my five brothers?'

" 'Ah, but they could read the warnings themselves,' Abraham said. 'Moses wrote about it and so did the prophets. They all tried to call the people back to God.' "

If only the rich man had chosen to change and obey God while he still had the chance. Now it was too late!

More Lessons about Prayer

Luke 18:1-8

Prayer is talking to God. Jesus wants us to talk to Him about everything. He wants to be our best Friend. God always hears our prayers.

Sometimes when we pray to God, it seems like nothing happens. It may feel as though He is not listening. That is not true. God always hears us. Sometimes, though, His answer to our prayers is wait. It is hard to keep on praying during those times. But that is exactly what Jesus wants us to do. He told this story to teach His followers that they should keep on praying and never give up, no matter what.

"There once was a bad judge who was not afraid of anyone. One day a poor woman asked him for help against someone who was trying to cheat her. At first the judge ignored her. She had nowhere else to turn. Again and again she begged this judge to help her.

"In the end he agreed. If this is how a bad judge acts, think how God will listen to you. He is full of love and always willing to help people."

Broken Homes

Matthew 19:3-11; Mark 10:2-9

Sometimes a husband and wife break up their home. They leave each other. This is what divorce means. Everyone feels hurt. Often children feel the most hurt.

When a mother or father moves out

296

of the home, many children feel as though it were their fault. But it isn't. They shouldn't blame themselves. Sometimes mothers and fathers choose not to live together. There can be many reasons for this happening, but the children are never to blame.

Jesus knows that divorce can hurt people. He also knows there are times when a husband and a wife don't want to live together. When Jesus walked the earth, one of the Pharisees asked Him, "Can a man divorce his wife for any reason at all?"

Jesus did not like the question. He said that God brought men and women together so the two of them could be joined together and become one. God did not want husbands and wives to break apart. The religious leaders asked why the rules said it was all right to divorce.

Jesus said, "Because of your hard and stubborn hearts, you were allowed to leave your wives! But that is not how God wanted it to be. When a man and woman choose to marry, they are supposed to stay together until death."

When Jesus' disciples heard this, they said, "But if that's the way it is, then sometimes it must be better not to marry at all!"

Jesus said, "You're right. Not everyone needs to get married. And marriage that lasts a lifetime is truly a gift from God."

Jesus was trying to protect families. And in protecting the family, He was taking care of the children.

Laat die Kindertjies na My toe Kom

Matteus 19:13-15; Markus 10:13-16; Lukas 18:15-17

Jesus is die spesiale Vriend van kinders. Hy het eenmaal vir sy dissipels gesê die engele van klein kindertjies is altyd in die hemel naby aan God. Omdat kinders so maklik vertrou, is hulle baie, baie spesiaal vir God. Hy beskou elke kind as 'n besondere skat.

Die ouers wat Jesus hoor preek het, het dit geweet. Daarom het 'n klompie van hulle op 'n dag hulle klein kindertjies na Hom toe gebring. Hulle het gevra of Hy sy hande op hulle sou sit en vir hulle sou bid.

Die dissipels het egter gesê: "Gaan weg. Kan julle nie sien die Meester het rus nodig nie? Moenie sy tyd mors nie. Hy het belangriker dinge om te doen as om met babatjies te speel!"

Jesus het kwaad geword en sy kop geskud. "Nee," het Hy gesê. "Moenie hierdie kinders wegstuur nie. Laat hulle na My toe kom."

Hy het na sy dissipels gekyk en die kinders gebruik om hulle meer oor sy koninkryk te leer. "Die koninkryk van die hemel behoort aan elkeen wat soos hierdie klein kindertjies glo en vertrou. Slegs hulle wat so nederig en afhanklik soos kinders is, sal by my koninkryk ingaan."

Toe het Jesus sy sterk hande uitgesteek en aan al die babas en die kindertjies wat rondom Hom gestaan het, se koppe geraak. Hy het hulle omarm en nader getrek. Hy het ook in hulle oortjies gefluister en hulle laat lag.

Die ma's het gelag toe hulle opgewonde kinders na hulle terughardloop. Die dissipels het dít wat hulle gesien het, baie geniet. Hulle het selfs geglimlag. Die kinders het, beter as enigiemand anders, geweet wat Jesus bedoel het toe Hy gesê het: "Kom na My toe."

The Rich Young Man

Matthew 19:16-22; Mark 10:17-23; Luke 18:18-23

One day a man asked Jesus, "Good Teacher, how can I enter the kingdom of God? I want to live forever."

Jesus knew the young man was very rich. He also knew the man had trained for many years to become a religious leader. Jesus told the young man something he already knew. "Follow the commandments."

The young man said, "I have been careful to follow all the commandments. Now I want to do more." This man wanted to make sure he was as close as possible to God.

Because of this Jesus loved the young man. He knew, though, there was one thing which stood between this man and God. He knew the young man loved his money and things more than anything else in the world. The man loved God, but he loved being rich even more.

So Jesus said, "You have missed one thing. If you want to become perfect, go and sell your things and give your money to the poor. Then you will have treasure in heaven. Come, follow Me."

When the man heard this, he became very sad. He lowered his head and turned away. He knew deep down that he had not given God first place in his life. He was not willing to give up his riches and follow Jesus. So he walked away, very sad.

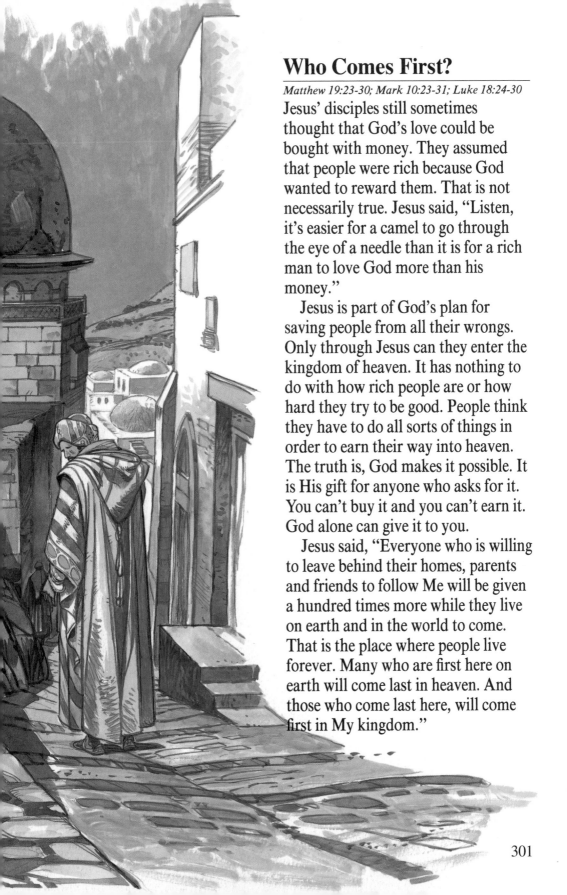

Who Comes First?

Matthew 19:23-30; Mark 10:23-31; Luke 18:24-30

Jesus' disciples still sometimes thought that God's love could be bought with money. They assumed that people were rich because God wanted to reward them. That is not necessarily true. Jesus said, "Listen, it's easier for a camel to go through the eye of a needle than it is for a rich man to love God more than his money."

Jesus is part of God's plan for saving people from all their wrongs. Only through Jesus can they enter the kingdom of heaven. It has nothing to do with how rich people are or how hard they try to be good. People think they have to do all sorts of things in order to earn their way into heaven. The truth is, God makes it possible. It is His gift for anyone who asks for it. You can't buy it and you can't earn it. God alone can give it to you.

Jesus said, "Everyone who is willing to leave behind their homes, parents and friends to follow Me will be given a hundred times more while they live on earth and in the world to come. That is the place where people live forever. Many who are first here on earth will come last in heaven. And those who come last here, will come first in My kingdom."

Die Werkers in die Wingerd

Matteus 20:1-16

Jesus het nog meer geleer oor hoe die laastes eerste sal wees, en die eerstes laaste. Dus het Hy vir sy dissipels hierdie verhaal vertel.

"Die koninkryk van die hemel is soos 'n man wat 'n wingerd gehad het. Hy het vroeg in die môre uitgegaan om werkers te huur. Hulle het ooreengekom op die gewone betaling vir 'n dag se werk. 'n Paar uur later het die eienaar nog meer mans gesien wat rondgestaan het met niks om te doen nie. Hulle was ook tevrede met die betaling wat die eienaar belowe het en het in die wingerd gaan werk.

"Die eienaar het weer, later die oggend, en die middag, vir meer werkers gaan soek. Hulle is ook na die wingerd gestuur. Kort voor die einde van die werkdag het die eienaar 'n laaste groep gevind. 'Hoekom het julle nie vandag iets nuttigs gedoen nie?'

"Hulle het geantwoord: 'Omdat niemand ons werk gegee het nie.'

"Die eienaar het gesê: 'Julle kan vir my werk. Gaan na my wingerd en help met die oes.'

"'n Uur later het die eienaar van die wingerd vir sy voorman gesê: 'Roep die werkers en betaal die laaste groep eerste.'

Die eienaar het die laaste groep wat gehuur is, eerste betaal. Hy het hulle 'n volle dag se betaling gegee, al het hulle net een uur gewerk! Toe het hy dié betaal wat tweedelaaste gehuur is, en so aan, tot hy by dié gekom het wat die hele dag gewerk het. Hy het vir elke werker dieselfde bedrag geld gegee.

"Dié wat eerste gehuur is, het gekla: 'Ons het gedink ons sal meer as hulle kry. Daardie mans het net 'n uur gewerk, terwyl ons die hele dag lank in die warm son gesweet het.'

"Die eienaar het gesê: 'Vriende, ek is regverdig. Julle het die betaling gekry waarop ons vroeër ooreengekom het. As ek my geld wil weggee aan ander wat minder as julle gewerk het, het dit niks met julle te doen nie. Julle het geen reg op meer geld nie. Ek kan met my geld doen wat ek wil. Neem wat julle s'n is en gaan huis toe.'"

Jesus het opgekyk na sy dissipels se vraende gesigte. "So sal die laastes eerste wees, en die eerstes laaste."

Al die mans is 'n volle dag se geld betaal, genoeg vir alles wat hulle nodig gehad het. Die werkers wat laaste gehuur is, was net so gewillig soos die ander om die hele dag te werk. So maak dit nie saak hoe ons na Jesus kom nie, Hy sal ons altyd vergewe. Hy wil vir almal van ons dieselfde geskenk van lewe in sy koninkryk gee. God hanteer ons almal dieselfde. Dit is ons geloof in God, en nie ons harde werk nie, wat ons in die hemel bring.

The Little Man in the Tree

Luke 19:1-10

In Jericho there lived a very rich man called Zaccheus. He was the top tax collector in that area. He made a lot of money for himself and for the Romans. Because of this, the Jews did not like Zaccheus. They called him a greedy traitor.

When Jesus was on his way to Jerusalem, he travelled through Jericho. Huge crowds lined the streets. They waited to see and greet Him with a big cheer. One man in the crowd was Zaccheus. He was so short he could not see over the crowd. So Zaccheus climbed a tree.

He pulled himself into the lowest branch. Then he stepped onto a higher one. He did not care if the people laughed at him up in the tree. He had heard the stories about Jesus being a friend of tax collectors. He just had to see Jesus, no matter what.

The people below him started cheering. Zaccheus saw a man come down the dusty street. "Is that Him? Ah, so that's Jesus of Nazareth!" Zaccheus said.

Zaccheus shouted with the rest of the crowd. Then suddenly, he stopped shouting. When Jesus passed beneath Zaccheus' tree, He looked up. He stared at Zaccheus. The tax collector could not say a word.

Instead, he just stared and stared. He had never seen eyes like Jesus' before. He could not tear his own eyes away. Jesus said to him, "Zaccheus, hurry and come down. Today I must stay at your house."

Zaccheus almost fell out of the tree. He was so surprised. He grinned. "What an honour!" he thought to himself. He scrambled down the trunk and led Jesus toward his home.

The people they passed on the way grumbled, "Look at that Jesus. There He goes again, staying with sinners."

When Zaccheus had welcomed Jesus to his house, he made a promise. "Here and now I promise to give half of whatever I earn to the poor. I'll also give back four times whatever I've cheated from others in the past." He bowed his head. Zaccheus knew who Jesus was. He was ready to change his life for Him.

Jesus said, "Today you and your family are saved. That's why the Son of Man has come here. I am here to save all the lost and hurting people."

Wysheid word Beloon

Lukas 19:11-27

Jesus het 'n ander verhaal vertel. "Daar was eenmaal 'n koning wat op 'n lang reis gegaan het. Voor hy by die huis weg is, het hy aan tien van sy slawe 'n groot klomp geld gegee. 'n Hele tyd later het hy na sy huis teruggekom. Hy het die tien slawe geroep en hulle gevra wat hulle met die geld gedoen het. Hy wou sien of hulle verstandig met die geld gewerk het of nie.

Al die slawe, behalwe een, het verstandig gewerk. Hy het die geld begrawe en nie probeer om meer te verdien nie. Die koning was baie kwaad. Hy het die geld van die man af weggeneem en dit vir die man gegee wat tien keer meer as die bedrag wat hy ontvang het, verdien het."

Jesus wou sy dissipels laat verstaan

dat dié verhaal oor hulle was. Hierdie mense het 'n kykie in die koninkryk van God gekry. Hy wou hê hulle moes weet dat diegene wat meer wil leer van die koninkryk van God, beloon sal word. Maar diegene wat hulle rûe draai op dít wat Jesus hulle gewys het, sal met minder as niks agtergelaat word.

Maria se Liefdesdaad

Matteus 26:6-13; Markus 14:3-9; Johannes 12:1-8

Jesus was vir die laaste keer voor sy dood, op pad na Jerusalem. Die laaste aand voor Hy by die stad ingegaan het, het Jesus by Lasarus, Maria en Marta gebly.

'n Snaakse ding het gebeur toe Marta daardie aand die kos bedien. Maria, wat Jesus van die begin af liefgehad en aanbid het, het iets baie besonders gedoen. Sy het baie duur parfuum oor Hom uitgegooi.

Maria het geweet dat Jesus binnekort sou weggaan. Dit was haar manier om te wys dat Jesus haar Koning was. Dus het sy die parfuum op Jesus se kop uitgegooi. Daarna het sy gekniel en die parfuum in Jesus se voete ingevryf en dit met haar hare afgedroog.

Die ander gaste het stil toegekyk. Niemand het beweeg nie. Die geur het die kamer gevul. Maar daar was mense wat nie gehou het van wat Maria gedoen het nie. Hulle het gedink Maria kon die parfuum verkoop en die geld vir die armes gegee het.

"Los haar uit," het Jesus gesê. "Sy het 'n pragtige ding vir My gedoen. Julle sal altyd die armes by julle hê en

julle kan hulle help wanneer julle wil.
Maar julle sal My nie altyd hier by
julle hê nie.

"Die verhaal van wat Maria vanaand
gedoen het, sal oor en oor vertel word.
Die mense sal haar nooit vergeet nie."

The Big Parade

Matthew 21:1-7; Mark 11:1-7; Luke 19:29-35; John 12:12-16

The morning dawned clear and bright. Jesus told His disciples, "Today we will enter Jerusalem." As He led them toward the city gates, an amazing thing happened. The crowd around Jesus became bigger and bigger and bigger! Hundreds and thousands of people poured out of the city to welcome Him. Cheering and shouting, they called Him the Son of David. It was a welcome fit for a king!

Just outside Jerusalem there was a wooded hillside called the Mount of Olives. When Jesus reached this place, He sent two of His disciples to get a donkey. They brought it back to him. Jesus rode into Jerusalem on a donkey.

Many of the people tore palm branches off the nearby trees. They waved the palms for Jesus. They saw Jesus as their king, one who might deliver them from the Romans.

But Jesus is not that kind of king. That is why He rode into the city on a donkey, instead of a general's stallion. He was trying to show the people that His was a mission of peace. He was the King, riding a beast of burden. The people in Jesus' kingdom are the burdened of this world. They are those who choose to come to Him and ask for help.

Jerusalem! Jerusalem!

Matthew 21:8-11; Mark 11:8-11; Luke 19:36-44; John 12:17-19

When Jesus entered Jerusalem, it seemed the whole city was shouting, "Hosanna to the Son of David!"

"Blessed is He who comes in the name of the Lord!"

Others yelled, "This is the prophet Jesus, from Nazareth in Galilee!"

The religious leaders were not so happy, though. "You see," they said to each other, "the whole world is following Him now."

They grew especially angry when the people shouted, "Blessed is the King who comes in the name of the Lord!"

"Make them stop calling You that!" they shouted at Jesus.

He turned and stared at them. "If I did that, the very stones of Jerusalem would shout the same. You cannot stop them!"

Then Jesus looked out over Jerusalem. Tears ran down His face. He was crying for Jerusalem, the City of David, the City of God. "Oh, if only you could believe what you see today. But you will become blind and your enemies will destroy you!"

Even as the people cheered Him, Jesus knew they would soon betray Him. He wept for the disaster their wrong choice would bring. He cried out of love for the very people who would soon scream for His death.

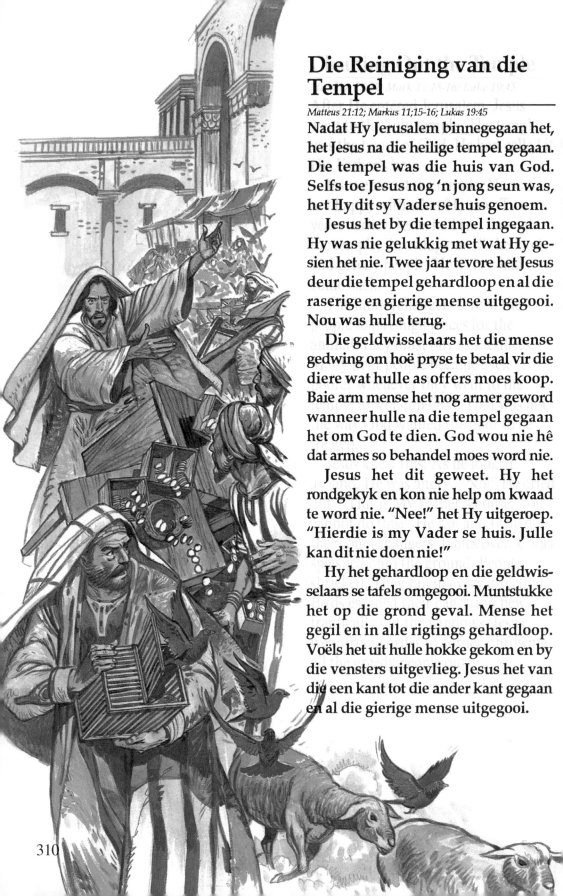

Die Reiniging van die Tempel

Matteus 21:12; Markus 11;15-16; Lukas 19:45

Nadat Hy Jerusalem binnegegaan het, het Jesus na die heilige tempel gegaan. Die tempel was die huis van God. Selfs toe Jesus nog 'n jong seun was, het Hy dit sy Vader se huis genoem.

Jesus het by die tempel ingegaan. Hy was nie gelukkig met wat Hy gesien het nie. Twee jaar tevore het Jesus deur die tempel gehardloop en al die raserige en gierige mense uitgegooi. Nou was hulle terug.

Die geldwisselaars het die mense gedwing om hoë pryse te betaal vir die diere wat hulle as offers moes koop. Baie arm mense het nog armer geword wanneer hulle na die tempel gegaan het om God te dien. God wou nie hê dat armes so behandel moes word nie.

Jesus het dit geweet. Hy het rondgekyk en kon nie help om kwaad te word nie. "Nee!" het Hy uitgeroep. "Hierdie is my Vader se huis. Julle kan dit nie doen nie!"

Hy het gehardloop en die geldwisselaars se tafels omgegooi. Muntstukke het op die grond geval. Mense het gegil en in alle rigtings gehardloop. Voëls het uit hulle hokke gekom en by die vensters uitgevlieg. Jesus het van die een kant tot die ander kant gegaan en al die gierige mense uitgegooi.

Genesing in die Tempel

Matteus 21:13-17; Markus 11:17-18; Lukas 19:46-48

Jesus het van die een kant van die tempel na die ander kant gehardloop. Hy het vir die geldwisselaars gesê: "God het gesê hierdie plek moet 'n huis van gebed wees. Julle het dit in 'n rowerspelonk verander!"

Toe Hy klaar was, het Jesus stilgestaan en rondgekyk. Die tempel was leeg, behalwe vir sy volgelinge en 'n paar ongelukkige godsdiensleiers. Stadig het blinde en kreupel mense weer by die tempel ingekom. Hulle wou hê dat Jesus hulle gesond moes maak. Weer en weer het Hy sy hand uitgesteek en siek mense gesond gemaak.

Die kinders wat hierdie dinge gesien het, het rondom Jesus gedans. Hulle het hande gehou en hulle stemme het teen die tempelmure weerklink. "Hosanna vir die Seun van Dawid!"

In plaas van 'n rowerspelonk, het die tempel 'n plek van vreugde geword.

Die enigste mense wat nie gelukkig was oor die veranderinge in die tempel nie, was die Fariseërs. "Luister na hierdie lawwe kinders," het hulle gesnork.

Jesus het geantwoord: "Het julle nie die deel van die Skrif gelees wat sê dat klein kindertjies en babas lof aan God sal bring nie?" Elkeen wat Hom daardie dag in die tempel gehoor het, was verstom oor sy wysheid.

311

Who Gave the Most?

Mark 12:41-44; Luke 21:1-4

Jesus went over to the part of the temple called the treasury. There, people came and put money in a special box. It was their way of giving back to God what He had given to them. At least that was the way it was supposed to be. But the religious leaders had turned the treasury into a place where the poor became poorer. There the rich looked very holy because they gave so much money. It was money they could easily do without.

Jesus and two of His disciples sat down and watched. They saw a poor woman, a widow. She had hardly anything. She did not put in great amounts of money like the rich had. Instead she dropped two very small copper coins into the box. These were hardly worth a penny.

"Did you see that?" Jesus asked His disciples. "The truth is, this poor widow put in more than all the other people added together.

"They gave just a little from what they had left over. They gave what they could easily afford. She gave all that she had left. When she gave those two coins, she gave all that she owned."

The poor woman had given out of love. She trusted God would honour her gift. She knew He would help her continue on, even after she had nothing left. She believed in God and loved Him enough to give back her last coin. Such trust is worth more than all the money in the world.

313

The Five Careless Bridesmaids

Matthew 25:1-13

It will be very important to be ready when the end of the world comes. To show His disciples this, Jesus told them a story. "There once were ten bridesmaids. They were supposed to be ready to welcome the bridegroom. They were part of a wedding party.

"Five of these girls were careless and five were wise. All ten girls were supposed to wait along the roadside for the bridegroom to come home. When the bridegroom passed by, they would light his way with the lamps they held.

"The five foolish girls should have known they would need extra oil. They had brought only enough oil to fill their lamps once. Each of the wise girls, however, had brought plenty of extra oil.

"They waited and waited all evening, but the bridegroom did not come. They all fell asleep because it was so late. Suddenly there was a shout, 'The bridegroom is coming! Light your lamps!'

"The wise bridesmaids lit their lamps. But the foolish girls had used up all their oil a long time ago.

" 'Can we borrow some of your oil?' they asked the wise girls.

"They just shook their heads. 'No. There would not be enough for all of us. Go and see if you can buy some from the shop.' The other girls ran as fast as they could to buy some more oil. But while they were gone, the bridegroom arrived.

"Those who were ready, went in with him to the wedding feast. The door was locked. When the other girls came back from the shop, they were too late.

" 'Open the door,' they called out. 'Bridegroom, let us in, please.'

"But the bridegroom said, 'I don't

know you. Go away.' Let this be a lesson then," Jesus said to His disciples.

He was teaching them that someday time would run out. No one could afford to say, "I'll change tomorrow." Time is not the sort of thing you can borrow from other people. If you wait too long to do something, then it is too late. Now is the time to make the choice for or against Jesus. Don't wait until tomorrow.

Judas

Matthew 26:1-5, 14-16; Mark 14:1-2, 10-11; Luke 22:1-6

These were Jesus' last few days before He was arrested. He spent much of that time with His disciples. He taught them, trying to help them understand what He had to do. The time had come for Jesus to make real all the words the prophets had told about Him so long ago.

Jesus was not the only one preparing for His death. The chief priests and other religious leaders could think of nothing else. "We'll have Him arrested without anyone noticing," they told themselves.

They also warned each other, "We must be careful not to do this during the Passover festival. There are a lot of people who think He is the Messiah. They might cause us trouble if they see Jesus being arrested." There were still two days to go before the Passover festival.

The religious leaders plotted about how they would capture Jesus. A man named Judas Iscariot arranged to meet them. They were very surprised. "Judas is one of Jesus' special twelve followers!" one leader said.

"Not only that, Judas is the disciple in charge of all the money," another said.

Judas met with them. He asked, "How much money will you give me if I hand Him over to you?"

The chief priests were delighted. They smiled and rubbed their hands together. "We will pay you thirty pieces of silver." That was the price of betraying Jesus to His enemies.

From that day on, Judas watched for a chance to trap Jesus. He would not have long to wait.

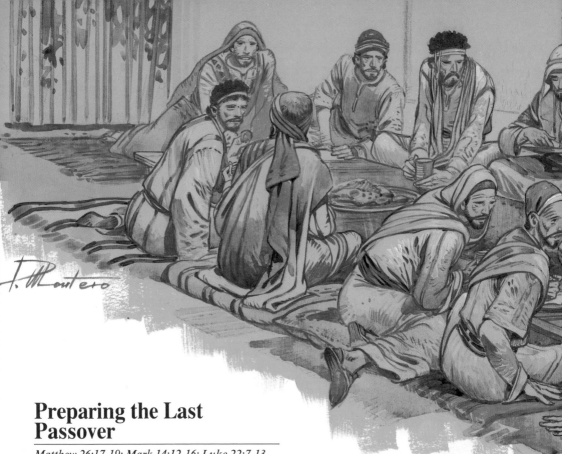

Preparing the Last Passover

Matthew 26:17-19; Mark 14:12-16; Luke 22:7-13

Two days after Judas made his deal, the Passover festival began. Thousands of people had come to Jerusalem for this.

On Thursday Jesus told Peter and John, "I want you to get everything ready for the Passover."

"But Teacher, where do You want us to do this?"

He said, "Go into the city. There you will meet a man carrying a jar of water. Follow him. Then go to the owner of whichever house this man enters. Tell the owner, 'The Teacher says His time has come. He would like to bring His disciples and keep the Passover at your house.'"

Peter and John did as Jesus said.

When they approached the owner of the house, he nodded. It was as if he had known all along that Jesus would stay at his home. Together, they made sure there was enough food in the house.

The man showed Peter and John a big room upstairs. There was a large, low table. Jesus and His disciples could share the Passover meal in private. It would be a meal like no other, one which would go down in history.

Who Is Greatest?

Luke 22:14, 24-30

That night Jesus and His twelve closest disciples would break the bread

and drink the wine of Passover. They remembered how God had saved His people in Egypt. He had destroyed the terrible pharaoh who had forced them into slavery.

Jesus sat quietly at one end of the table. A few of the disciples talked together. Their heads were bent close. Suddenly, this little group started arguing. "I am!"

"No, I am!" They were fighting about who was the greatest, the most important disciple. Some thought it was John and some thought it was Peter.

Jesus frowned and spoke. "Kings and rulers fight over power. You must be different. With you, the one who serves should be your leader.

"Who is more important? The one who sits at the table eating, or the one who serves the meal? With you it is the one who serves the meal. Look at Me, I'm serving you. This is how you should be with each other. You have stayed with me; when all this is over, you will join Me in My Father's kingdom. Then you will sit on thrones and judge the twelve tribes of Israel."

319

The Servant King

John 13:1-9

Jesus looked around at His twelve closest friends. These were the men who would carry on His work after He went back to heaven. He loved these men. He had loved them from the beginning. He loved them to the end.

Jesus knew the Father had given Him a choice. As all people can, the Son of Man could choose to follow the plan God had for His life. Or He could turn away from the plan and go His own way. Jesus came from God. He wanted to return to God. He would always be at God's side. He looked around at His disciples and stood up.

The disciples stopped talking. They watched as Jesus poured water into a bowl. Then He looked up at them.

"My friends," He said. "No one has washed your feet." He went to each one of them and knelt. Then Jesus slipped off their sandals and washed their feet. He dried them with a towel He had tied around His waist.

Jesus was Teacher and Leader to these men. Yet He was doing something only a slave was supposed to do. With His own two hands and a bowl of water, He slowly cleaned the sand and dust off each of the men's

feet.

Peter could not stand it anymore. He cried out, "Lord! What are You doing? Lord, are You going to wash my feet, too? That's a slave's job!"

"You don't understand now why I'm doing this. Someday you will," Jesus said.

Peter answered, "No! Never! You should never have to wash my feet!" Peter could not bear to see Jesus, their King, acting like a slave.

"Peter, if I don't wash you, you can't grow any closer to Me."

When Peter heard this, he said, "Not just my feet then, Lord. Please wash my hands and my head, too." Even then Peter did not fully understand what Jesus was doing and why.

The Reason Why

John 13:12-18

When Jesus had finished, He put His robe back on. He sat down again. Then He told them the reason why He had acted as their slave.

"Do you know what I was doing? You call Me Teacher and Lord, and you are right. If I, who am your Lord, wash your feet, what do you think you should do for each other?"

The disciples had been fighting about which of them was the greatest. Now He said, "I've given you an example to follow. This is the way to become truly great.

"Anyone who believes what I say to you, is not just believing in Me, but also in My Father who sent Me." The ones who follow Jesus' example, are doing what God wants.

Jesus knew His disciples would need as much help as possible in sorting out the next few days. A dark time was ahead of them all. If they could learn to serve each other, the dark time might be a little easier to get through. They would have the Lord's blessing, if only they chose to listen and hear.

The Lord's Supper

Matthew 26:20-29; Mark 14:17-25; Luke 22:14-23; John 13:18-27

At the Passover meal Jesus told His disciples, "I'm going to be betrayed by one of you!"

The disciples gasped. Who would turn the Teacher over to His enemies? They looked at each other and wondered, "Is he the one?"

Jesus said, "I'm going to dip this piece of bread. Whoever dips his bread with Mine is the one." Then Jesus dipped the bread. Judas, the son of Simon Iscariot, joined Him. God's enemy went into Judas then. Jesus said, "Go and do what you must."

Judas got up and left the room. The other disciples thought he might be going out to buy more food. Judas knew he was going to Jesus' enemies.

Jesus took a loaf of bread and tore it into pieces. He handed the chunks around the table. He thanked God for it and said, "Eat it. This is My body. Remember Me when you do this."

Then Jesus took the cup of wine. He lifted it up high. He thanked God again. Then He said, "This is My blood to take away sin. Drink from this, all of you. I will always be with you. I won't drink this again until I drink it with you in My Father's kingdom."

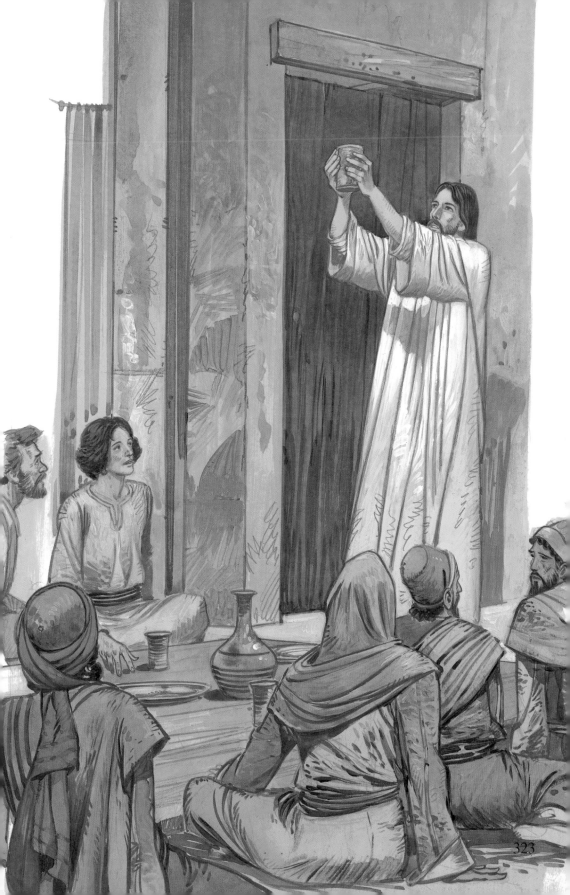

When the Cock Crows

Matthew 26:30-35; Mark 14:26-31; Luke 22:31-34; John 13:31-38

Jesus had changed the Passover feast into "The Lord's Supper." This was Jesus' last meal on earth. The Last Supper would become a very special way for Jesus' followers to remember Him.

He and His disciples had finished the meal. They stood and sang a very old song of praise to God. Then it was time for them to leave the house. Jesus headed for the Mount of Olives. This was a quiet place with old trees. It was a place to rest and think, a place to pray. It was a place to wait.

Jesus and His disciples climbed the hill to the garden which was called Gethsemane. As they walked, Jesus said, "Tonight, you will all run away. No matter what happens, remember that I'll meet you in Galilee afterwards."

Peter said, "No! Maybe the others will desert You, but I won't!"

"Peter," Jesus said, "before tonight is over, that is exactly what you will do. Before the cock crows three times at dawn, you will have sworn three times that you don't even know Me."

"Oh no! I'd sooner die than do that!" Peter cried out.

The other disciples said the same. "We'll never run away!"

A Home in Heaven

John 14:1-6

The disciples were very upset. They followed Jesus and tried to make sense of what Jesus had been telling them.

"All evening long He's talked about His being betrayed and dying. What does it all mean?"

"Did you see how upset the Teacher was while we ate? Do you really think He's going to die soon?"

"I don't know," another answered. "I don't see how. Look how quiet everything is. Everyone is at home."

"What if He does go away? What will we do then?"

Jesus knew they were confused and afraid. He said, "Listen, you must stop worrying like this. You've been trusting God, now trust Me. When I die, I am going back to My Father. There is a place for everyone in heaven. I will prepare a place for you. I will come back and take you home with Me. Then we will always be together."

One of the disciples, Thomas, said, "But Lord, we don't know where

You're going. How will we ever get there?"

Jesus said, "I am the way, and the truth, and the life. The only way to reach the Father, is through believing in Me." Jesus doesn't just show us the way to God, He is the Way to God!

Jesus Prays for His Followers

Matthew 26:36-46; Mark 14:32-42; Luke 22:39-46; John 17:1-18:1

On the way to the garden, Jesus stopped. He wanted to pray with His disciples one last time.

He said, "Father, the time has come. You gave Me these men. They listened and believed that You sent Me. For their sakes, keep them safe after I leave. While I was with them, I guarded them. Now I go to You so they can have more joy than they ever dreamed possible.

"The world may hate them, but You and I love them. Let them be one, as We are. As they go into the world now, be with them, as You were with Me. Let the love You gave Me, now live inside them."

Jesus was asking the Father to protect all His followers for all time. He was praying for people like you and me. When He had finished, He led them into the garden.

There, He took Peter, James and John. They went off alone together. Jesus was very upset. He said, "My soul is torn up inside, to the point of death. Stay here and keep watch." He was going to talk with His Father. Then He said, "Pray that you won't be weak tonight." Jesus went off by Himself to pray.

A short distance away from the disciples, He fell onto the ground. "Oh, Father!" Jesus cried out. "If it's possible, don't let Me go through this pain. My Father, isn't there any other way, must I go through this?" Jesus knew God wasn't making Him do anything. Jesus had chosen to obey. That way God could work miracles. He could offer all people for all times a chance to start again and be clean with God.

Jesus looked up at the stars. He said, "Father, I'm willing to do what You want."

Then an angel from heaven came to Jesus. The angel made Him stronger. Jesus prayed and prayed. The sweat pouring down His face was like drops of blood. Each one left a mark in the dust as it fell onto the ground.

Finally He stood up and went back to His disciples. They had fallen asleep! They were so sad and confused. They just curled up and went to sleep. "Peter, are you asleep? Couldn't you even keep watch for one hour? Stay awake with Me and pray that you won't be tempted tonight."

This happened two more times. Jesus went off to pour His heart out to God. He came back, only to find the disciples fast asleep. It was a lonely time for Jesus. When He came back the third time, He said, "Are you still sleeping? All right. The time has finally come. Look! Get up! Let's go. Look! There he is, the one who betrays Me!"

Betrayed by a Kiss

Matthew 26:47-50; Mark 14:43-46; Luke 22:47-48; John 18:2-9

Jesus warned Peter, James and John. Then they heard voices at the far end of the garden. The disciples looked up. They saw many lights coming their way. They were suddenly very afraid.

Peter saw the religious leaders. They carried clubs and swords. "His enemies!" Peter gasped at John. Then he hissed, "Look!"

There was Judas! Peter asked, "Why would Judas be talking to our enemies?" Peter already knew the answer.

Judas had just told the religious leaders, "Arrest the man I kiss. I'll show you who he is." Judas headed toward Jesus. "Teacher!" he called out.

"Judas," Jesus said, "are you betraying the Son of Man with a kiss?" Judas could not look Jesus in the eye. He hugged the man who had been everything to Him, Teacher, Friend, God. Then Judas turned away without looking back.

In a flash, the chief priests and elders grabbed Jesus. He did not even struggle. "I am the One you are looking for. Now let these others go," Jesus said. He meant the rest of His disciples.

Jesus stood alone on that darkest of dark nights.

Peter Fights Back

Matthew 26:51-56; Mark 14:47-50; Luke 22:49-53; John 18:10-12

Peter could not believe Jesus' enemies were taking Him away. He rushed toward the angry mob. He waved his sword. Peter yelled, "Get back! Leave the Teacher alone!"

He struck out at the nearest person. With a mighty "Swish!" the sword cut off a slave's ear. This man worked for one of the chief priests. Peter stared at the ear.

"Stop it!" Jesus cried. "Put your sword away. People who hurt others end up getting hurt themselves!" Then Jesus touched the slave's ear and healed him.

He said to Peter. "If I had wanted to fight back, I would ask My Father to send thousands of angels to fight for Me. If I did that, I would not be doing what My Father wants. Don't you see? If you fight them, I can't do what I came here to do."

Then Jesus turned to His enemies. "There was no reason for you to take me this way, with swords and clubs. I'm not a thief. I've been teaching in the temple every day. You could easily have arrested Me there."

When the guards moved in, Peter and the other disciples ran and hid. They were afraid of being arrested with Jesus.

Jesus Is Taken Prisoner

Matthew 26:57; Mark 14:53; Luke 22:54; John 18:13-14

When Peter and the others ran away, Jesus was left alone with His enemies. It took a few moments for them to realize Jesus was not going to fight. Then they pushed Him. Jesus stumbled as they led Him away from the garden.

The guards brought Jesus to the high priest's house. There, all of Jesus' enemies met together. They put Him on trial. They had paid Judas to help them arrest Jesus. Now they wanted Him dead.

Peter's Great Mistake

Matthew 26:58, 69-75; Mark 14:54, 66-72; Luke 22:54-62; John 18:15-18, 25-27

Peter had followed behind the crowd who took Jesus. He was too scared to help. When he saw Jesus being taken into the high priest's house, he waited. The courtyard was full of soldiers. Some of the men had built a fire to keep themselves warm.

As Peter sat down by the fire, a servant girl came up to him. She stared at him. " You're one of the prisoner's friends."

Peter hoped no one had heard her. "No! No!" he said loudly. "I don't know what you're talking about."

Then he went out to the gateway. There another girl saw him. She said, "This man was with Jesus of Nazareth."

"No! No, you must be thinking of someone else. I don't even know the man!" After a little while, a group of men came up to Peter. One of them knew the man whose ear Peter had sliced off. "You're one of His followers, I saw you with Him in the olive garden just a few hours ago."

"Yes, he's from Galilee, all right. His accent gives him away," another man said.

Peter's heart beat faster and faster. He swore and shouted loudly, "I don't even know the man!"

No sooner were the words out of Peter's mouth, when he heard a rooster crow. Jesus turned and looked straight at Peter. Then Peter remembered what Jesus had said to him, "Before the cock crows, you will say you don't even know Me three times." Peter cried and cried over what he had done.

Jesus and Pilate

Matthew 26:59-68, 27:1-2, 11-14; Mark 14:55-65,
15:1-5; Luke 22:63-23:5; John 18:19-24, 28-38

The religious leaders were trying to prove Jesus had broken the Law. They even paid people to lie about Jesus.

The high priest asked, "Tell us in the name of the living God, tell us if

You are the Christ, the Son of God."

"Yes, I am," Jesus said. "One day all of you will see Me sitting on a throne next to God."

"He says He's God! That's against the Law!"

"Kill Him! Kill Him!" They struck Jesus. Then they spat in His face. Together with the soldiers, they beat Him up.

When the sun rose, the religious leaders took Him to the governor. This was a man named Pontius Pilate.

"What has He done?" Pilate asked the religious leaders.

They lied to Pilate. "This man makes the Jews fight against the Romans. He says He's a king."

"Are You the King of the Jews?" Pilate asked Jesus.

"If that's what you think," Jesus said. "But My kingdom is not of this world. If it were here, My followers would fight for Me. Yes, I am a king. I came to bring truth to the world. Everyone who loves the truth is My follower."

This gave Pilate something to think about. "Don't You hear the terrible things they say about You?" Jesus did not say a word. Pilate was amazed. He said, "I can't find any reason to have this man killed. He hasn't done anything wrong."

The religious leaders said, "He's come all the way from Galilee just to cause trouble."

Jesus and Herod

Luke 23:6-12

"What did you say?" Pilate asked the religious leaders. "Did you say this man was from Galilee? If that's right, then He should be judged by Herod. He's in charge of that area, not me."

Pilate did not want to have anything to do with Jesus. "He's done nothing wrong," he told himself. Pilate watched the guards take Jesus to Herod.

It just so happened that Herod was in Jerusalem at that time. He was there to see the Passover festival. When Herod saw Jesus, he was very pleased. He had wanted to meet the strange man everyone was talking about. "Maybe He will even work some miracles," Herod thought.

Herod was disappointed. He asked Jesus many questions. Jesus gave him no answers. The religious leaders stood there the whole time, yelling and shouting at Jesus.

"He's a dangerous criminal!"

"He calls Himself the Messiah!"

"You should kill Him!"

Herod grew tired of Jesus' silence. He and his soldiers joined the religious leaders. They made fun of Jesus. They dressed Him in a long robe. They sneered, "Ha ha! A fine king You would make now!"

"Send this fool back to Pilate!" Herod ordered. "Stop wasting my time. Get Him out of here!"

So Jesus returned to Pilate. It was

very strange. Before that day, Pilate and Herod had been enemies. They were two Romans, fighting each other for more power. After they both saw Jesus, they became the best of friends.

337

Pilate Tries to Free Jesus

Matthew 27:15-18; Mark 15:6-11; Luke 23:13-17; John 18:39

Pilate was not happy when he saw the guards bringing Jesus back to him.

Pilate knew Jesus had done nothing wrong. The religious leaders were jealous of how popular He was with the people. Pilate thought about it and thought about it. Then he had an idea! There was one way he could set Jesus free. It just might work. . . .

At every Passover feast the governor could let one prisoner go free. The people chose which prisoner they wanted. Pilate hoped that this year the people would choose Jesus.

There was one other prisoner the people could choose to let free. His name was Barabbas. He was a murderer, a very bad man. When the crowd was ready, Pilate asked them, "Who do you want me to set free, Barabbas, or Jesus?"

The Death Sentence

Matthew 27:19-26; Mark 15:12-15; Luke 23:18-25; John 18:40

While Pilate waited for the crowd to decide, his wife sent him a message. "Be careful! Don't let them kill Jesus. I had a terrible dream about Him last night. I've been worried ever since."

The religious leaders had posted their men throughout the crowd. "Ask for Barabbas!" they told all the people. "Tell the governor you want Jesus to die!"

Pilate ordered both Jesus and Barabbas to stand in front of the people. "So which man do you want me to set free?" he asked again.

"Barabbas!" they yelled.

This took Pilate by surprise. "What should I do with Jesus?"

"Crucify Him!"

"Why? What has He done wrong?"

They shouted all the louder, "Crucify Him! Crucify Him!"

Pilate tried three times to talk the people out of hurting Jesus. "There's

338

no reason to kill this man. Why don't
you let me just punish Him, then set
Him free?"

The crowd yelled even louder,
"Crucify Him!" They were getting
ready to riot! Pilate called for a bowl
of water. He washed his hands. "I
have nothing to do with this man's
blood," he said. "This is something all
of you have done!" The people agreed.

Pilate let Barabbas go free. He had
Jesus whipped, then handed Him over
to be crucified.

They Make Fun of Jesus

Matthew 27:27-31; Mark 15:16-20; John 19:1-16

The crowd had told Pilate they wanted Jesus killed. Pilate ordered Jesus to be brought inside the palace.

The soldiers crowded around Jesus. They pushed Him one way, then the other. They took off His clothes and put a robe on Him. The robe was the colour worn by kings, a reddish-purple. The soldiers did this so they could make fun of Jesus.

"Look at Him! Now He doesn't look like a king!"

"A king should have a crown!"

They twisted together a crown of thorns. They forced it onto His head. They put a stick in His right hand and knelt in front of Him. The guards laughed at Him.

"Long live the King of the Jews!" they sneered. They spat on Him and took the stick. They hit Him on the head with it again and again! All the while, Jesus did not fight back.

The soldiers led Jesus back to Pilate. He tried again to tell the religious leaders there was no reason to kill Jesus. As soon as the priests and religious leaders saw Jesus, though, they shouted, "Crucify Him! Crucify Him!"

"You crucify Him! I can't find any reason to have this man killed!"

"He says He's the Son of God," they answered back. "And according to Jewish Law He must die for this!"

Pilate went back inside the palace. "Where do You really come from?" he asked Jesus. Jesus said nothing. Pilate said, "Don't You know I have the power to set You free?"

Jesus shook His head. He said, "You have no power over Me. God is in control here."

Pilate tried one more time to set Jesus free. The people still would not let him.

The Weeping Women

Matthew 27:32-33; Mark 15:21-22; Luke 23:26-31; John 19:17

The soldiers forced Jesus to take up two heavy pieces of crossed wood. As they climbed the hill, Jesus stumbled and fell. The soldiers told a man named Simon to carry the cross for Jesus.

A group of women had followed Jesus up the hill. They wept for Jesus. He turned to them. "Don't cry for Me. Cry for Jerusalem. This city has turned its back on the Messiah."

Jesus on the Cross

Matthew 27:34; Mark 15:23; Luke 23:36

Jesus could barely stand, He was so weak. The cruel whip had torn open His back. Blood ran down His face from the crown of thorns.

One of the soldiers went up to Jesus. He forced Him to drink some drugged wine which might ease the pain. After tasting it, Jesus shook His head no.

Then the soldiers stretched Jesus onto the cross. They nailed His hands and feet to the wood.

343

The Last Moments

Matthew 27:35-43; Mark 15:24-32; Luke 23:34-38; John 19:18-27

They nailed Jesus to the cross. Above His head they hammered a sign. "This is the King of the Jews." A soldier made fun of Him. Even as he hung on the cross, the soldiers gambled to see who would get Jesus' robe.

Some of the people shouted up at Him, "If You are the Son of God, come down from the cross!"

Not everyone standing around Jesus' cross wanted to hurt Him. Among the women were His mother and another Mary and Mary Magdalene. Jesus saw His mother and John standing next to each other. He

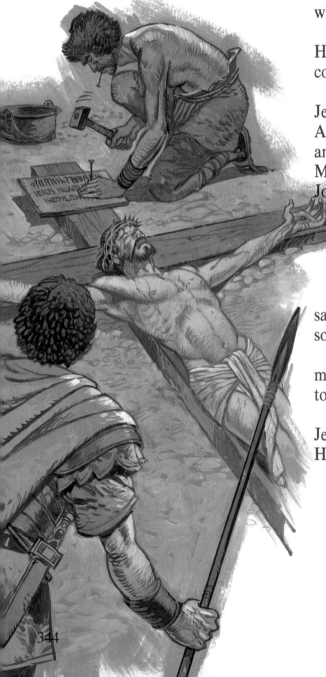

said to her, "Mother, this man is your son now."

Then He said to John, "This is your mother now." From that day on, John took care of Mary, Jesus' mother.

Even up to the very last moments, Jesus took care of those who loved Him.

344

The Death of Jesus

Matthew 27:44-50; Mark 15:33-37; Luke 23:39-46; John 19:28-30

The crosses of two other men stood near Jesus. Both were robbers. One robber laughed at Jesus. "Save Yourself and us! You're supposed to be the Christ, aren't you?"

The other robber said, "You should be more afraid of God. This man has done nothing wrong." Then he called out, "Jesus! Remember me when You come in Your kingdom!"

Jesus said, "I promise. Today you will be with Me in paradise."

After Jesus was hanging on the cross for six hours, He cried out, "My God, My God, why have You left Me so alone?"

During those hours on the cross, Jesus became the go-between for people and God. Jesus is the Way through which any man, woman or child can be touched by God.

That afternoon, the whole earth was covered with darkness. Like a blanket, the heavy blackness covered both city and countryside.

Jesus was also in darkness. For the first and only time in Jesus' life, God looked away from His Son. As Jesus took on the sin of the world, He felt the pain and hurt of it all.

Jesus said nothing for a long time. He was in great pain and very slowly dying. "Father, here is My Spirit!" Jesus had suffered enough. The price was paid. The way back to God was

346

347

open now.

Then Jesus cried out again with a loud voice, "It is finished!" It was a cry of a battle won. Jesus bowed His head and took His last breath. Jesus was dead.

The Temple Curtain Splits in Two

Matthew 27:51-54; Mark 15:38-39; Luke 23:45, 47-49

The very moment that Jesus cried out, He gave up His Spirit to heaven. The curtain in the temple split in half. This curtain marked the way into the holiest place of the temple. This was the closest anyone could get to God. Only the high priest was allowed in, and then only once a year.

A very special thing happened when the curtain split in two. When Jesus died, it meant people no longer had to wait for the high priest to pray for them to God. Jesus had died for all people. He made a Way for them to reach God. So there was no need for the curtain any more. Anybody could reach out to God, thanks to Jesus.

Jesus had died. The sky was dark. There was a great rumbling noise. The earth shook. Huge stones split and fell from the hills. Stranger and stranger things happened that evening when Jesus died.

"Why is it so dark?" people screamed.

"It's the end of the world! We're being punished!"

Men and women cried out in fear. They ran. Panic gripped the city. Many of the tombs, or places where dead people were buried, opened up. Dead bodies became alive. Later, these people would walk around Jerusalem as if they had never died.

The Burial

Matthew 27:54-60; Mark 15:39-46; Luke 23:49-54; John 19:38

The Roman captain and his men could not believe their eyes! The wind whipped around the captain. He had seen how Jesus had died. That was not the way any normal man died. He looked for the sun, but could not find it. "There's no doubt! This was the Son of God!" The captain said, "I've never seen anyone die like that!"

After six hours of hanging on the cross, Jesus was dead. A group of women helped a rich man from Arimathea, named Joseph, take Jesus off the cross. They knew that in a few hours the Sabbath would begin. Then nobody would be allowed to do any work. They would not be allowed to bury the body then.

So Joseph took the body down. He wrapped it in a clean linen cloth. Mary Magdalene and the other Mary were with him, together with more women. They slowly carried Jesus' body into the tomb which Joseph had bought for himself. Now the cave, carved out of rock, would be for Jesus.

351

Guards at the Tomb

Matthew 27:61-66; Mark 15:47; Luke 23:55-56;

John 19:39-42

Joseph laid the body of Jesus in his tomb. He and the rest of Jesus' friends wrapped the body in a linen cloth. They placed spices between the folds. The women had wanted to rub special creams onto the body of Jesus, but time was running out. When the sun set, they had to leave. They all wept. Their hearts were heavy with sadness. Jesus was dead.

Jesus' body lay safe in the tomb. The religious leaders went to Pilate. "Sir," they said, "Jesus said He would come back to life again after three days. Please order the cave to be sealed and post a guard. Otherwise His disciples might come and steal the body. Then they could say to the people, 'See, He has risen from the dead.' This last lie would be worse than all the rest!"

Pilate told them, "Very well, you can have some of my soldiers to guard the tomb. Now go and make sure the tomb is shut tight."

They closed off the cave. They posted a Roman guard, then sealed the stone. While they were doing that, they thought to themselves, "Now there's no way anyone can steal the body. There's no way they can say He rose from the dead. We've made sure of that!" But these religious leaders were in for quite a surprise.

353

An Empty Tomb

Matthew 28:1-8; Mark 16:1-8; Luke 24:1-10;
John 20:1

It was the morning after the Sabbath.
It was still dark as the women made
their way to the tomb. Mary
Magdalene and the others had been
waiting for this moment. Now they
could finally return to Jesus' tomb and
anoint His body.

One woman asked Mary
Magdalene, "But how will we ever
move the huge stone? How will we get
inside the cave?"

"I don't know," Mary sighed.
"We'll find a way, we have to."

Just as the sun dawned, the women
arrived at the edge of the garden. They
held their pots of perfumes and
precious ointments. As the sun peeked
over the horizon, the women moved
closer to the tomb.

Suddenly, the ground shook. It was
an earthquake! The soldiers Pilate had
sent to guard the tomb were thrown to
the ground.

An angel of the Lord came down
from heaven.

The angel moved to the opening of the tomb. He rolled away the stone covering the entrance. He sat on top of it. The angel shone like lightning. His clothes were as white as snow.

"Don't be afraid," the angel said to the women. "There's no need to be frightened. I know you're looking for Jesus. He isn't here. He's come back to life again, just as He said He would. Come in and see where His body used to be." The angel stretched out a long arm toward the women. He invited them to enter the tomb.

Mary Magdalene placed the ointments on the ground. She stood up. She took the hand of one of the other women. "Come on," she whispered. "We have to go and look."

They slowly entered the cave. "Oh no!" Mary Magdalene cried out. "He's gone! They've taken Him away!"

"No one has taken Him. Jesus is alive! Yes, He's risen from the dead," the angel answered. "Now hurry and tell His disciples He will meet them in Galilee. Make sure that Peter hears the news."

The women ran away from the tomb as fast as they could. They went off in different directions. They had never felt so happy and scared at the same time before.

355

Mary Magdalene Sees Jesus

Mark 16:9-11; Luke 24:12; John 20:3-18

Mary Magdalene ran back to tell Peter and the rest of Jesus' followers the good news. He and John went back with her to the tomb. It was empty, just as she had said.

Mary Magdalene had watched as they went inside. She had seen them enter the tomb with looks of fear on their faces. And she had seen them come out with looks of excitement and confusion.

When the men went home to wait, she stayed by the tomb. She stood outside and cried. She felt so afraid. Was the message from the angel for real? She thought that someone might have stolen the body. Mary Magdalene did not at all understand what was happening.

Jesus had died. But now His body was gone from the tomb. What did it all mean?

As she cried, Mary Magdalene happened to bend over and look inside the tomb. Suddenly, she saw two men dressed in shining white clothes sitting where the body of Jesus had been! They said to her, "Dear lady, why are you crying?"

She said, "I'm crying because they've taken away my Lord. I don't know where they've put Him."

Then she turned around and saw Jesus standing behind her in the garden. But she did not know it was Jesus. He was somehow different. He said to her, "Dear woman, why are you crying? Who are you looking for?"

Mary Magdalene thought the man standing in front of her was the gardener. She said, "Sir, if you have carried Him away, tell me where you have put the body. I will take Him away."

In that soft but strong voice of His,

Jesus said to her, "Mary!" At the sound of her name she quickly turned around. Then Mary saw who He was. Only Jesus could say her name like that.

"Oh Teacher!" she cried and fell at His feet.

Jesus said to her, "Don't touch Me yet. I still need to go up to the Father. Instead, go to My brothers. Tell them I said, 'I am going back to My Father and your Father, My God and your God.'"

Mary ran back to the disciples. This news she shared with them was even more exciting than what she had told them before. "I've seen the Lord!" She told them all that He had said.

The Disciples See Jesus

Mark 16:14-16; Luke 24:36-48; John 20:19-21

Soon after this, Jesus appeared to His followers. They had been hiding in a house when Jesus Himself suddenly appeared out of nowhere!

"Peace be with you!" Jesus said. The disciples were very frightened. They had locked all the doors. Since no one could enter, they thought Jesus must be a ghost. He told them they should have believed the stories told by Mary Magdalene. He was disappointed that they had not believed.

Then He said to them, "Why are you so frightened? Why do you doubt what is in your hearts? Look at My hands and My feet. Touch Me and see.

A ghost doesn't have flesh and bones like I have!" Then Jesus asked for something to eat. He wanted to prove He was no ghost.

He told them everything was happening just as it was written long ago. The books by the prophets, Moses and King David had said this would happen.

"You have seen all these things. Now go into all the world and tell them what has happened. That will be your greatest job."

Jesus left the room. The disciples looked at each other in wonder. It was all too good to be true! Yet it was true. Jesus had risen from the dead! He was with them again!

359

The Story of Thomas

John 20:24-29

When Jesus appeared to the disciples, one of the eleven was missing. This was a man named Thomas.

After Jesus was gone, Thomas came back to the room where everyone was hiding. When he entered, the disciples told him, "Thomas, oh Thomas, it is true! We've seen Jesus! He's alive!"

He said to them, "No. I won't believe it unless I see the nail marks in His hands. I have to put my finger where the nails were. If I can put my hand into His side, then I'll believe you."

Eight days later, Jesus visited the disciples again. This time Thomas was with them. Jesus walked right through the locked doors. He stood in the room. "Peace be with you," He said.

Then He said, "Thomas, come here with your finger and see My hands. Touch the wounds in My hand. Put your hand into My side. Stop doubting now and believe."

Thomas felt very ashamed for not believing. He hung his head, "My Lord and my God!"

Jesus answered him, "Is it because you have seen Me, that you now believe? There will be many who do not see and are still willing to believe. Those people are special to Me."

Jesus was talking about people like you and me. Do you believe or are you like doubting Thomas?

Breakfast by the Sea

John 21:1-14

At another time, Jesus appeared to His disciples at the Sea of Galilee. One evening, Peter said to six of the other disciples, "I'm going fishing."

"We'll come, too," they said.

All night long they fished. They threw the net over one side, then over the other. No matter where they fished, the net always came back empty. Finally, the long night of wasted work was over. When the sun was just coming up, the men decided to come back to shore.

As they neared the beach, they saw

a man waving at them. "Hello there!" He called out. "Have you caught any fish?

"No, not even one!" they shouted back.

"Try again! Throw the net over the right side of the boat. Then you'll find some!" The men did as He said. They were amazed! The net was so full, they could not even haul the catch on board.

John looked toward the shore again. He gasped at Peter, "It's the Lord!" When Peter heard this, he dived into the sea. Peter swam as hard as he could toward the beach. The other disciples brought the boat in. They dragged the net behind them. As they came closer, they saw Jesus already had a fire burning. He was cooking fish and warming bread for them.

"Bring Me some of the fish you've just caught," He said.

When the others came ashore, Peter helped them drag the net onto the beach. As he did so, he was astonished at the catch. Over a hundred fish strained against the net, yet it did not tear.

Then Jesus said to them, "Come and have breakfast."

Do You Really Love Me?

John 21:15-19

That morning Jesus helped the disciples catch a net full of fish. After they had eaten, He stayed and talked with the disciples.

Jesus called Peter over to His side.

362

"Peter, do you really love Me? Do you love me more than these other men do?"

"Yes, Lord. You know that I love You," Peter replied.

"Feed My lambs," Jesus told him. Then He asked the same question again, "Peter, do you really love Me?"

"Yes, Lord. You know that I love You."

"Take care of My sheep," Jesus said. A third time He asked, "Peter, do you love Me?"

Peter felt sad when Jesus asked him the same question three times. He could still remember that terrible night when Jesus was arrested. Three was the number of times Peter had told others that he knew nothing about Jesus. He sighed. "Lord, You know everything. You know that I love You."

"Feed My sheep," Jesus answered. It would be Peter's job to lead the disciples of Jesus. He would be one of the leaders in the years to come.

Home to the Father

Mark 16:19-20; Luke 24:50-53; John 14:1-2; Acts 1:3-11

Jesus appeared several times to His disciples after He rose from the dead. He worked miracles. He taught them to do all the things they had been learning about. A month after He died and rose again, Jesus left earth and went to heaven.

Jesus led His disciples outside of Jerusalem to Bethany. This was where His friends Lazarus, Martha and Mary lived. All His followers were around Him. He lifted His hands and blessed them. Then He told them to go straight back to Jerusalem. They should wait there for what the Father had promised.

Jesus said, "John baptized with water. You will be baptized with the Holy Spirit not many days from now. You will receive power when the Holy Spirit has come upon you. You will be My witnesses here and even to the farthest corners of the earth."

Then, an amazing thing happened. Jesus was taken up to heaven! He rose higher and higher until He disappeared into a cloud. The disciples looked at each other. They had seen one miracle after another. Now this had been the greatest of all! Jesus, crucified then risen, now taken up to heaven to be with His Father.

Jesus' disciples stared at the sky. Then two men dressed in white came and stood beside them. "Men of Galilee, why are you looking into the sky? Jesus has gone from you into heaven. He will come back again in the same way He left."

They went back to Jerusalem full of joy. They went straight to the temple and sang praises to God. Some wondered about this place Jesus had gone to, heaven. They remembered He had said, "Don't worry. Believe in God, believe also in Me. In My Father's house are many rooms. Soon I will go and make them ready for you." And that is why Jesus went back to heaven.

A Time of Waiting

John 15:26; 16:7; Acts 2:1

When Jesus had visited His disciples, He said, "Someday I will send you the Helper. He is the Spirit of truth who comes from the Father. He will help you to believe in My plan for your lives."

Later He added, "It's really much better for you that I go away. If I don't, the Helper won't come to you. I promise I will send Him to you."

The "going away" Jesus had been talking about was His going home to the Father. Now Jesus had done that. The disciples were waiting for the Helper, or Holy Spirit. Jesus had promised He would come.

The disciples were afraid of being arrested. They knew the religious leaders could still cause a great deal of trouble for them. They had found a way to crucify Jesus. They might find a way to hurt His followers, too.

So the disciples waited. They waited for ten days. They waited and wondered what would happen. What would this Helper do? Who was He really?

The Helper

Acts 2:1-13

One day, as the disciples were hiding, they heard a noise like a great wind. The noise did not come from outside the room, but inside! It filled the

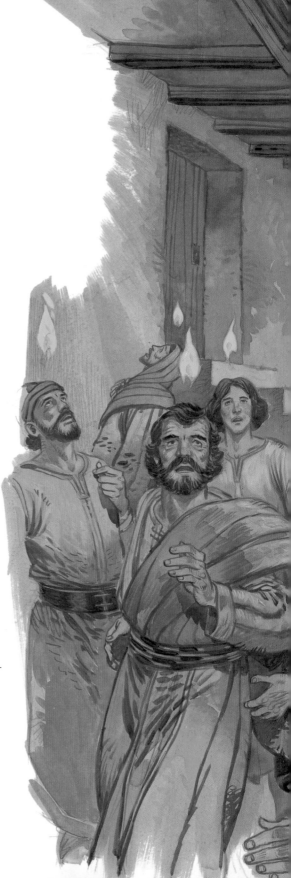

whole house. Suddenly, small flames appeared in the air. The flames hovered over each one of them.

They were being filled with the Holy Spirit! Their time of waiting was over. They opened their mouths and started speaking languages they had never studied or spoken before. This was a special gift from the Holy Spirit. Now people could hear about Jesus, no matter where they came from.

At that time Jerusalem was filled with people from many different countries. There were people from Africa and all over Europe. They spoke many different languages. When the disciples went outside, the other people heard them. The crowd was amazed. "What was that strange sound we heard?"

"You heard it too? It sounded like a mighty wind."

"Hey, listen to those men talking!" someone else in the crowd called. "How is it possible? These men all come from Galilee, but they speak like we do."

The Holy Spirit had stripped all fear from the followers of Jesus. They no longer huddled together in an attic room, too scared to open the door. Instead, they poured onto the streets. They laughed and talked all at the same time. They made no secret of their faith in Jesus. They told everyone they met all about Him.

Healing and Teaching

Acts 2:43; 3:1-10

With the Holy Spirit's help, the apostles could do miracles. More and more people were believing in Jesus, so the church was growing every day. One time Peter helped make a beggar better. This man had never been able to walk.

Peter and John passed him on the temple steps. The beggar tried to ask for money. Instead, the two apostles wanted to give him much more.

"I don't have any money," Peter told him. "What I do have, I give to you. In the name of Jesus Christ of Nazareth, walk!" Peter took him by his right hand. He helped him up to his feet. Straight away the beggar felt his legs become stronger. He stood up by himself!

"I can walk! I can walk! Blessed be the God of Israel!" the man shouted. He jumped and danced into the temple, following Peter and John.

Peter and John in Trouble

Acts 3:11-4:22

The people at the temple were astonished to see the beggar jumping up and down. A crowd soon gathered.

Peter saw all the people wondering what had happened. He said, "This was really Jesus who healed the man, not us. We only did it in Jesus' name. You had Jesus killed. God brought Him back to life again. He is the Messiah. By believing in Him this man has been made better."

This made the religious leaders very angry! They did not like anyone talking about Jesus. They called the guards and had Peter and John arrested. "That will keep them from talking about this Jesus coming back to life," the religious leaders told each other. They had Peter and John thrown into jail for the night, but many more people believed.

The next day the religious leaders called for Peter and John. They asked the two apostles how they had healed the crippled man. Peter was filled with the Holy Spirit, so he answered with wisdom.

The religious leaders said, "These men have never been to any schools. They're just simple people from Galilee. How can they talk so well? Listen!" they told them. "If you agree to stop talking about this Jesus, we'll let you go."

"What do you think is right? To do what God wants, or to do what you want? Do you think God wants us to listen to you or to Him?" Peter answered. "We can't stop talking about what we've seen and heard." Peter and John were not at all afraid of the religious leaders. There was nothing more the priests could do. The man Peter had healed was standing right in front of them. So they let Peter and John go.

An Angel Frees the Apostles

Acts 5:12-20

Each day the apostles met at one of the temple gates. They talked to the crowds about Jesus. Many believed them and became followers of Christ. Others were scared of getting into trouble. They did not get too close, but listened anyway.

The religious leaders grew angrier and angrier about all of this. They were very jealous. They did not want to ever hear about Jesus again. Yet more people were believing in Him than ever! How was it possible?

Finally, they ordered the guards to throw the apostles into prison. During the night God sent an angel of the Lord to them. He opened the prison door and said, "Go your way. You are free. Go back and tell all the people at the temple about the new life in Jesus."

The Apostles Are Questioned

Acts 5:21-42

The apostles went back to the temple, just as the angel had told them. In the morning the chief priests heard the apostles had escaped. Now they were even more worried than ever.

"Those men you're looking for are talking to people at the temple,"

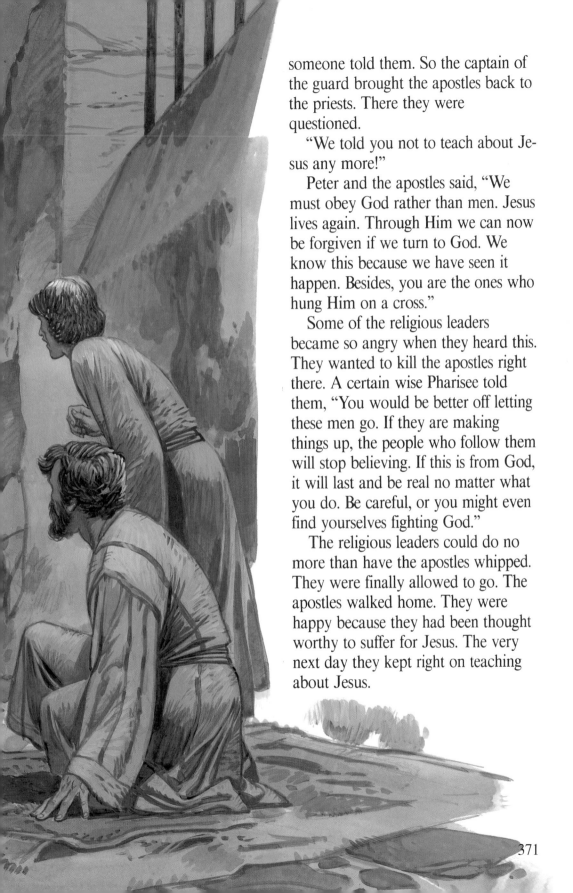

someone told them. So the captain of the guard brought the apostles back to the priests. There they were questioned.

"We told you not to teach about Jesus any more!"

Peter and the apostles said, "We must obey God rather than men. Jesus lives again. Through Him we can now be forgiven if we turn to God. We know this because we have seen it happen. Besides, you are the ones who hung Him on a cross."

Some of the religious leaders became so angry when they heard this. They wanted to kill the apostles right there. A certain wise Pharisee told them, "You would be better off letting these men go. If they are making things up, the people who follow them will stop believing. If this is from God, it will last and be real no matter what you do. Be careful, or you might even find yourselves fighting God."

The religious leaders could do no more than have the apostles whipped. They were finally allowed to go. The apostles walked home. They were happy because they had been thought worthy to suffer for Jesus. The very next day they kept right on teaching about Jesus.

Stephen Is Not Afraid

Acts 6:1-7:60

More and more people believed what the apostles were teaching. They wanted to find out about Jesus. They had chosen to follow Him. They had put Him first in their lives. As this happened, though, some practical problems came up. One problem was making sure some of the widows received their fair share of food.

The apostles chose seven men to take care of the problem. This gave the apostles more time to talk to people about Jesus. All seven of these men were full of faith and the Holy Spirit. One of them was called Stephen. He was very close to God. He did his job very well and God worked miracles through him.

There were some men who tried to argue with Stephen. They could not. There was no way they could match the wisdom of God's Spirit. These bad men found some people to lie about Stephen.

"Stephen has said bad things about

372

Moses and God." Before long, more and more people joined the religious leaders. They made sure Stephen was arrested.

He was brought before a court. Stephen was not even a little worried. His face shone like an angel's. The religious leaders did not care if Stephen had never done anything wrong. They tried everything they could to get him in trouble. They brought in people who lied about Stephen. This is what they did when Jesus was on trial, too. They twisted the words he had spoken about Jesus. This was very wrong, of course.

Stephen was filled with the Holy Spirit. God's Spirit helped Stephen know what he should say and when. He answered all their questions with great wisdom. Finally he said, "You have chosen not to listen to what God wants. Didn't your fathers try to kill the prophets? Now look at you! You have killed the Messiah. He came to save you!"

The religious leaders were furious. Stephen looked up. He saw Jesus sitting next to God the Father in heaven. He said, "Look, I see the sky opening up. There is the Son of Man!" He pointed upwards.

The crowd went crazy. They covered their ears and rushed at Stephen. They drove him out of the city. Then they threw stones at him. He fell to his knees and cried out, "Lord Jesus, take my spirit! Lord, don't hold this against these people!" Then Stephen died. He died a hero for Jesus, a man of courage and wisdom.

The Road to Damascus

Acts 8:1-4; 9:1-8; 22:4-11; 26:9-18

When Stephen died, there was one religious leader who liked what he saw. He was called Saul. Saul had wanted Stephen dead as much as any of the other religious leaders. Stephen's death marked the beginning of a terrible time of suffering for Jesus' followers. It was also a time when God's people showed great courage. Over and over again, people chose to die for what they believed. They did not turn their backs on Jesus. Many believers were forced to leave their homes and run for their lives.

The enemies of Jesus had hoped to kill off His followers. Instead they only made them stronger. The number of believers grew as they scattered. They ran away from bad men like Saul. As they ran, they told people that Jesus was worth living . . . and dying for.

Saul plotted about ways to kill Jesus' followers. He hated anyone who had anything to do with Jesus. His hatred was very dangerous and ugly.

Saul went to the chief priest. He asked if he could search for Jesus' followers inside and outside the country. Then he would arrest them all. He wanted to bring all of Jesus' followers back to Jerusalem. No matter if they were men or women. He would have them killed.

Word that Saul was on his way spread fast. All the believers in the area prayed for each other. They knew Saul was more terrible than any other. He was cruel.

Saul went to Damascus first. He carried important letters. These gave him the right to arrest any of Jesus' followers. Armed guards travelled with him. As Saul travelled in that direction, though, a truly amazing thing happened! Suddenly, a light from heaven flashed around him. It knocked Saul off his horse!

Saul fell to the ground. He heard a Voice say to him, "Saul, Saul, why are you hurting Me so much?"

"Who are You, Lord?"

"I am Jesus of Nazareth. Through My followers you keep arresting me. Through them you put Me into prison. You kill Me over and over again. Now get up and go into the city!"

The men who were with Saul heard the Voice too. They saw no one. Saul did as he was told. When he opened his eyes, he found he was blind! He had his men lead him to the place Jesus had told him to go. There he waited in darkness.

A Sheet Full of Animals

Acts 10:1-16

The Good News about Jesus was spreading. Many people chose not to listen. Many risked their very lives and believed. The time had come, though, for more people than just the Jews to hear the Good News.

Many times in Jewish history, God had spoken through His prophets. He had said how there would come from the Jewish people a Light. This was Jesus. The Light would save the world. Even Jesus had said His teaching was at first for the Jews. Later it would be for people from all over the world. This was one of the reasons why the religious leaders had hated Him so much. They liked being God's only chosen people. Now the time had come for all that to change. God made this clear through two men, Peter and a man named Cornelius.

Cornelius was not a Jew. He was a Roman centurion, or army officer. He was in charge of over one hundred Roman soldiers. Even so, he and his whole family believed in the one God. Cornelius was a man of prayer. He often gave his money to the poor.

One afternoon Cornelius was praying. He had a vision. He saw an angel who called out, "Cornelius!"

"What is it, Lord?" he stared at the angel. He felt afraid.

"God has heard your prayers. He is pleased with all your gifts to the poor. He is ready to answer you. Now send

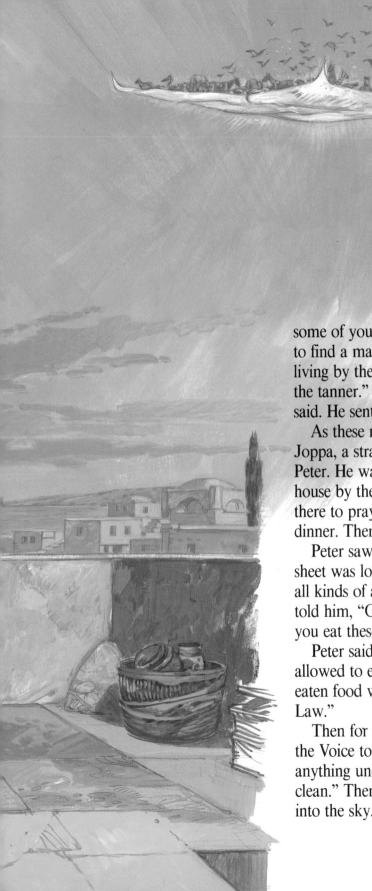

some of your men to Joppa. Tell them to find a man named Peter. He is living by the sea in the house of Simon the tanner." Cornelius did as the angel said. He sent three of his men.

As these men were heading for Joppa, a strange thing happened to Peter. He was sitting on the roof of the house by the sea. He had gone up there to pray while waiting for his dinner. Then Peter had a vision, too!

Peter saw the sky open up. A great sheet was lowered down. Inside were all kinds of animals and birds. A Voice told him, "Get up, Peter. It's all right if you eat these animals!"

Peter said, "Oh no, Lord, we're not allowed to eat these things. I've never eaten food which is unclean by our Law."

Then for a second and third time, the Voice told him, "Don't call anything unclean that God has made clean." Then the sheet was lifted back into the sky.

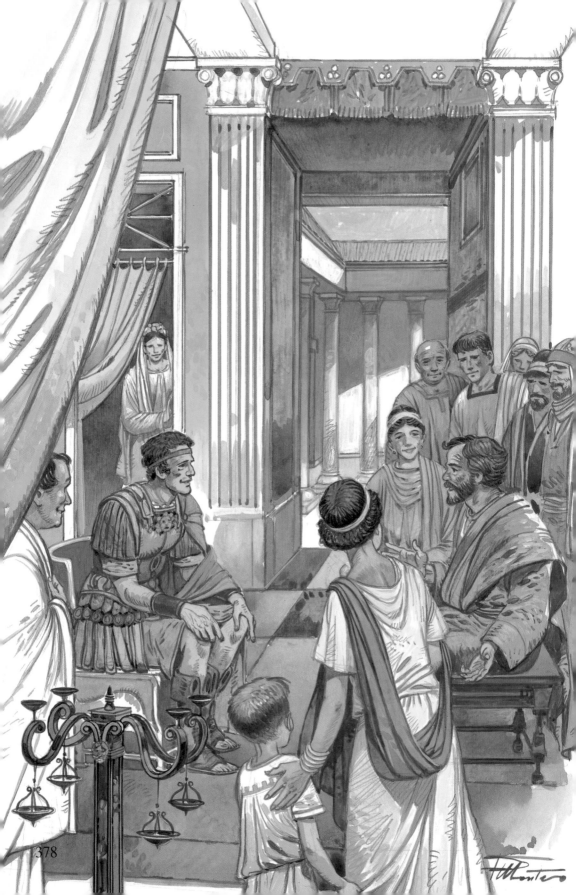

Peter Visits an Army Officer

Acts 10:17-48

When Peter woke up from his strange vision, he was very confused. "What does it mean?" he wondered. Then God's Holy Spirit told Peter, "Get up now and go downstairs. Three men are looking for you. Don't worry, I have sent them."

Peter went downstairs. He heard from the three men how an angel had told Cornelius to send for Peter. So the next day he set out. Peter travelled with some other believers from Joppa. Peter arrived at the house. Cornelius fell at his feet and bowed down before Peter. All his friends and family were there. They heard Peter say, "Please get up. I'm just a man like yourself."

Peter took a good look around the room. It was full of men, women and children. Most of them were not Jews. He said, "You know yourselves that it's against Jewish Law for me to visit you. Yet God has shown me that He loves everybody, no matter if they're a Jew or not. That's why I'm here. Now why did you send for me?"

Cornelius said, "I'm so glad you've come to my house. I had a vision that we should send for you. God has something to tell us through you. Did He give you a message?" He told Peter what the angel had said to him during the vision. Peter nodded.

"Yes, He did. Listen, God treats everyone the same. There is no difference. He welcomes everyone who believes in Him. I see that now."

Suddenly, while Peter explained this, the Holy Spirit swept through the room. He came upon everyone who was listening. They all began speaking in tongues and praising God!

The Jewish believers Peter had brought with him were surprised. They had never seen the Holy Spirit come upon non-Jews.

Good News for Everyone

Acts 11:1-26

News of what had happened quickly reached the other apostles. Non-Jews, or Gentiles, had received the word of God! Some of the apostles were not very happy about it. They thought Peter had broken Jewish Law for mixing with non-Jews. The time had come for the whole world to become God's family. As soon as Peter came back to Jerusalem, they questioned him.

"You broke the Law," the apostles said. "You stayed at the home of Gentiles. You even ate with them!"

Peter explained exactly what had happened. He told them about his vision and the angel who had visited Cornelius.

When the other apostles heard this, they stopped grumbling and praised God. "This means that God has given everyone the chance to turn to Him and start new lives in Jesus."

It was at this time that the believers were first called "Christians." It meant "belonging to Christ."

Peter Escapes from Prison

Acts 12:1-17

More and more people listened and believed Jesus' followers. This was sometimes very dangerous. The evil King Herod wanted to kill all the Christians.

Many of the Christians were forced to run away. Some had to live in caves to meet secretly. Not everyone got away. Herod did catch Peter. Herod threw him into prison and ordered four squads of soldiers to guard him. "After the Passover we will put him on trial," King Herod said. But God had other plans.

Peter was not alone. Many people were praying for him. Peter wasn't afraid to die. He could still hear the words Jesus had said so often to him, "Don't be afraid." He thought about this during the night before his trial. Peter was chained to two soldiers. There were also guards in front of the door.

Suddenly, an angel of the Lord filled the prison cell with light. He shook Peter, "Get up quickly." Peter stood up. The chains fell right off him! "Put on your sandals and coat. Then follow me!" the angel said.

Peter did as he was told. He did not believe it was really happening. "I must be dreaming," he thought. One by one, they passed the guards. No one even looked at Peter! When they reached the gates into the city, they opened all by themselves! Peter stepped out onto the street. The angel disappeared.

Peter made his way to a house where the Christians were meeting that night. When Peter knocked at the door, a servant answered. She heard Peter's voice. The servant was very happy it was Peter. She ran to tell the others, but forgot to open the door! "It's Peter outside!"

The others looked up. "What? Well, maybe it was his angel."

All this time, Peter was knocking and knocking on the door. They finally opened it and everyone started talking at once.

Peter calmed them down. Then he told them how the Lord had let him out of prison.

Paul as a Preacher

Acts 9:10-25; 14:1-22

Saul was blind when he arrived at
Damascus. By the time he left, he
could see again, both in his eyes and
heart. Saul became one of Jesus'
strongest followers. He also changed
his name. Now he was called Paul.

Paul travelled from village to village.
He told people his story. He was a
religious leader who had wanted to
kill all Christians. Then God had met
him and changed him. Jesus had
forgiven him. Paul wanted nothing
more than to tell people how Jesus
could change lives.

Sometimes Paul travelled with
friends. One of these was a man
named Barnabas. Together they went
from city to city. They taught the
same things Jesus had taught.
Sometimes they made friends and
sometimes they made enemies.

In one place they met a man who
had never been able to walk. This man
listened to Paul with all his heart. Paul
said, "Stand up!" The man jumped up
and could walk! He was so happy, he
started dancing!

Later, some Jews from Antioch told
many people that Paul was evil. They
beat him up. They threw rocks at Paul
until they thought he was dead. Then
they dragged him outside the city.
While the disciples stood around his
body, Paul got up and went right back
into the city to preach, as if nothing
had happened!

383

Singing in the Prison

Acts 16:16-34

One day, Paul and his friends healed a young girl. She was a slave who could tell other people's fortunes. While she was sick, her masters had made a lot of money from this. When Paul made her better, her masters could not make any more money. They grew angry. So they grabbed Paul and Silas and dragged them to the police.

They lied about them and called them traitors. An angry mob beat up Paul and Silas. They threw the two

men into prison. Paul and Silas had their feet fastened between heavy blocks of wood. They were chained and put under heavy guard.

They were chained in one position. They could not even move around a little bit. Their backs ached from the beating the guards had given them. It looked like a hopeless time for the two apostles.

Paul and Silas did not give up. They did not complain. Instead, they sang! At about midnight, they sang and prayed, praising God. The other prisoners listened to them. Suddenly, a great earthquake shook the prison! The cell doors swung open. Everyone's chains came undone.

The jailer woke up and saw all the doors open. He drew his sword and was about to kill himself. He thought all the prisoners had escaped. He knew his punishment would be terrible. Paul cried out, "Don't hurt yourself! We're all still here!"

The jailer called for lights. He rushed in and trembled with fear. He fell down before Paul and Silas. Then he led them out of the prison. He asked, "Tell me, please, how do I become a follower of your God?"

Paul and Silas said, "Believe in the Lord Jesus and you will be saved." The jailer nodded.

Then he brought Paul and Silas to his own home. There he washed their wounds. The rest of the family listened to Paul talk about Jesus. They wanted to become Christians, too. The jailer and his family were all baptized right there. Then they served a meal to the apostles. Everyone was filled with joy because they knew what it meant to believe in God.

Paul Is Warned

Acts 20:17-38

Paul was on his way back to
Jerusalem. He tried to teach in as
many places as possible. Many years
had gone by since Paul first was
blinded on the road to Damascus.
Now he visited old friends and made
new friends. He wrote many letters to
those friends he could not visit in
person.

Paul wanted to reach Jerusalem as
quickly as possible. He knew he would
not see his friends again. They warned
him that Jerusalem would be
dangerous. He said, "You know I must
go on to Jerusalem. I must finish the
work God has given me to do. Be
careful while I'm gone. Watch out for
people who would like to see all our
hard work ruined. Protect the Church
here and carry on the work God has
given us."

Over and over again, Paul's friends
warned him about all the people who
wanted him killed. Jerusalem had
been the most dangerous city for
Jesus. It would be the same for Paul.
Everyone knew Paul would probably
be thrown into prison there. Even Paul
knew that. It did not matter. He still
had to go where God wanted him.

Paul wrote all this down in the
letters he sent to friends. They were
glad to hear from him. Everyone
worried, though. What would happen
to Paul in Jerusalem?

386

Paul Speaks to the Mob

Acts 21:27-23:11

Jerusalem did turn out to be a dangerous place for Paul. The religious leaders led the people in a riot. They tried to kill Paul. Roman soldiers arrived just in time, though. They arrested Paul, so the crowd would not kill him.

They did not know who he was or what he had done wrong. Paul asked if he could talk to the crowd. The soldiers agreed.

Paul asked the people to listen to him. Then he told them who he really was. He told how Jesus had changed him from an enemy of the Christians into one of their leaders. He talked about how he had met Jesus on his way to Damascus. Then God had sent him out to preach to the non-Jews, as well as the Jews.

When the crowd heard this, they stopped listening and started yelling. "Away with him! Kill this man!" The commander brought Paul inside the fort. He was about to beat him so he could find out what he had done wrong.

"Wait a minute!" Paul warned him. "Are you allowed to beat a Roman citizen without a fair trial?" The soldiers could get into a lot of trouble if they hurt Paul without a good reason. So the commander talked to the religious leaders in the crowd. The captain would bring Paul to them the next day to be tried.

At his trial Paul tried to explain again. Nobody listened, though. Everyone started shouting at everyone else. The troops kept Paul from being torn to pieces. That night, Paul was back in prison. The Lord stood next to him. "Be brave, Paul. You're doing the right thing. Just as you told people about Me here in Jerusalem, so you must tell them in Rome."

Paul Must Die!

Acts 25:1-26:32

As a Roman citizen, Paul was supposed to get a fair trial. Instead he had to spend two years in prison.

The Roman governor was called Festus. He said, "I think you should come to Caesarea." So for the fourth time, Paul was put on trial. This time, his enemies were there with him. They accused him of one crime after another. But no one had any proof. Festus did not want to get into trouble with the religious leaders.

Paul told Festus, "You're the governor. If you can't judge me, then don't hand me over to my enemies. They tell nothing but lies about me. I appeal to Caesar."

Paul was claiming his right as a Roman to be tried by Emperor Nero himself. It meant that, no matter what, he would not be turned over to the religious leaders. But he also would not be let free until Nero had seen him.

Festus did not know what to do with Paul. He had no choice but to make sure he went to Rome. There he would be tried by the emperor. But before he let Paul go, Festus asked King Agrippa what he thought of the case.

Once again, Paul told what happened. This time he stood in front of the son of King Herod and many other very important people. When he had finished, Agrippa said to him, "Do

you think you can talk me into becoming a Christian so easily?" Then he turned to Felix. "This man has done nothing wrong. In some ways it's too bad he asked to see Caesar. Now we

can't let him go free. He must go to Rome."

Shipwrecked!

Acts 27:1-26

Paul was finally on his way to Rome. It was not in the way he had thought he would go. He was not travelling as a free man, on his way to visit friends. Paul was under heavy Roman guard, a prisoner. He was on his way to see Emperor Nero.

One of the soldiers in charge of Paul was an officer named Julius. He could see that Paul was not dangerous. He treated him kindly. When Paul was put on board the ship to go to Rome, Julius said Luke and some of Paul's other friends could travel with him. They changed ships, going from port to port. Over and over again they ran into bad weather. Finally the storms made sailing almost impossible. The little ship carrying Paul had found a harbour on the island of Crete. Paul told them, "If we don't stop here for the winter, we'll not only lose the cargo, but our lives as well." The owner of the boat was in a hurry to deliver his cargo of grain to Rome. He did not listen to Paul and they sailed on.

Before long, a very strong wind caught the ship! There was nothing the crew could do. For more than a day, the storm tossed the ship. Waves swamped its decks. The crew threw the cargo overboard.

The sky was dark for many days. The captain could not see the moon or stars. They were lost at sea! All the crew were terribly seasick. No one had eaten for a long time. Paul told them, "Men, be brave. None of you will die. Last night an angel of God told me I would stand before the emperor. None of you will die. Instead, we will land on an island."

Safe in Malta

Acts 27:27-28:10

All of a sudden there was a terrible grating sound. The boat ripped open on the rocks! It started breaking up. "Jump ship!"

The waves crashed all around them. Each man made it to the beach safely. That was all that mattered. Once on shore, they found out the island was Malta. They were close to Italy, after all. The people who lived there were very kind. Paul was safe and he would go to Rome after all.

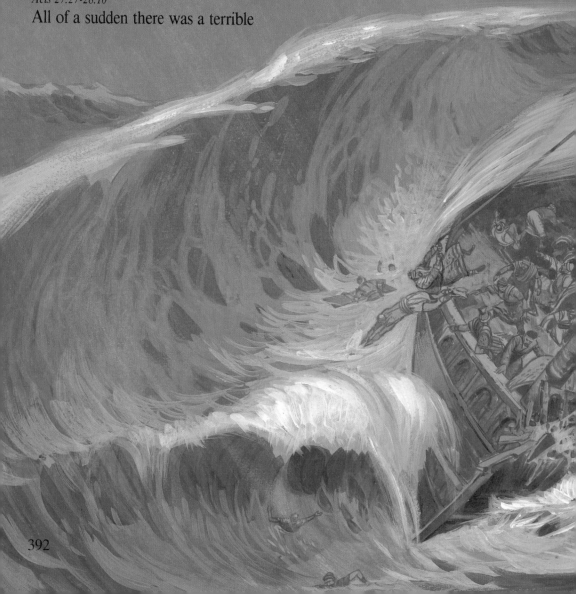

393

Rome at Last

Acts 28:11-31

Paul finally did arrive in Rome.
Believers from all over the area came
to meet him and Luke and the others.
When Paul saw them, he thanked
God. He felt brave again.

The Romans did not put Paul into

prison this time. They let him go where he wanted. This was all right, as long as a soldier went with him. Paul went to the religious leaders in Rome. He told them what had happened. They said, "We haven't heard anything about you from the Jews in Jerusalem. Come and tell us more."

Once again Paul told how Jesus had met him on the road to Damascus. He told how he had travelled all over, telling people about Jesus. He told them how he met Jesus and how Jesus changes lives. He told how God had sent His Son for Jews and non-Jews. "I haven't done anything wrong," he finished.

The Jews didn't know what to think. Some believed Paul. Others were not so sure. For the next two years, they would fight about Paul. In the meantime, Paul waited until the emperor would see him. The Romans let him go where he wanted, as long as his guard stayed close by. Paul used this time to preach and teach. He welcomed everyone. No one tried to stop him.

Those two years would be the last chance Paul ever had to preach freely. Some people think he spent part of that time going to Spain and then Greece. Later he was arrested again and put back into prison. There, he wrote letters to many of the friends he had met while preaching. Paul was finally killed by Emperor Nero in Rome.

Special Messages

Revelation 1:1-3:22

When the apostle John was a very, very old man, he had a vision. It was like a great dream. Jesus asked John to write down the dream.

John saw Jesus standing in front of seven golden lampstands. John wrote that Jesus' eyes were like blazing fire. His voice was like the sound of rushing water. Jesus's face was like the sun shining on the brightest of days.

Jesus told John to warn the Christians. Some had forgotten what was most important. "You do not love Me as you did in the beginning." The poorer churches were rich in love. Those who suffered for Christ would be rewarded in heaven.

Jesus also sent a warning to some churches. They had become blind to their own problems. "Those of you who think you can take care of yourselves, are foolish. If you think it is better to rely on yourselves, rather than on God, you're wrong."

Jesus told John to remind the Christians over and over again. They should love, give, turn to God and be faithful.

God's New World

Revelation 17:1-22:21

God's new world will begin when
Jesus comes back to earth. Those
who have followed Jesus will come
from all times and places. Jesus will
bring together the young and the old
and especially the children.
Everyone who knows Jesus and has
put their trust in him will be there.

399